THIS IS
COUNTRY

THIS IS
COUNTRY

A Backstage Pass to the
ACADEMY OF COUNTRY MUSIC AWARDS

WRITTEN BY LISA LEE

FOREWORD BY REBA McENTIRE

With contributions by

Marty Stuart, Loretta Lynn, Randy Owen, Garth Brooks,

George Strait, Blake Shelton, Luke Bryan, and Bob Romeo

INSIGHT EDITIONS

San Rafael, California

CONTENTS

REBA McENTIRE

I love awards shows. I always have. When one was over, I lived for the next one! You'd think they're all alike, but they're not. The Academy of Country Music Awards are different because Dick Clark mixed country music stars with movie and TV stars. That made it a lot more interesting for me because I love movies and TV, and I know this mix has to appeal to the fans, too.

The Academy of Country Music Awards were first held in 1966, honoring the industry's accomplishments from the previous year. It was the first country music awards program held by a major organization. In the beginning, the Academy wanted to promote country music in the Western states. At the first official ceremony held in 1966, Buck Owens won Top Male Vocalist, and Bonnie Owens won Top Female Vocalist. Merle Haggard was named Most Promising Male Vocalist, Kay Adams was named Most Promising Female Vocalist, and Buck Owens' band, the Buckaroos, was named Band of the Year.

The awards were first televised in 1972 on ABC. In 1979, the Academy and dick clark productions joined forces, with Dick Clark and Al Schwartz serving as producers and Gene Weed directing. Under their guidance, the show moved to NBC and finally to CBS, where it remains today.

My first ACM show was in 1981 in Los Angeles. I was nominated for Top New Female Vocalist along with Kim Carnes, Terri Gibbs, Sissy Spacek, and Sylvia. Terri had her huge hit out that year, "Somebody's Knockin'." She won, and I was hooked on awards shows. That was when it was held at Knott's Berry Farm in Los Angeles. It moved over to the Universal Amphitheatre, and then, in 2003, the show left LA and moved to Las Vegas.

A few years after my first appearance on the ACMs, Dick Clark asked if I'd be interested in cohosting with Mac Davis and John Schneider. Would I?! You dang right I would! That started my long stint hosting the ACM Awards, which became one of the events I most looked forward to all year. I also cohosted with George Strait and Randy Owen, with Randy Travis, and another year with Hank Williams Jr. There were several years where I hosted by myself, but I can honestly say that Blake Shelton had to be the most fun cohost. My straitlaced face and his little naughty fourteen-year-old-boy attitude proved to be a winning combination. We hosted together for a couple of years, then I passed the torch over to Luke Bryan to join Blake in all the fun. And what a fantastic team they make!

The hardest thing about being a host or cohost for the ACM Awards was not learning my lines or knowing when to enter or exit—it was having four different wardrobe changes (and that was on a light night)! And there was sure to be the occasional wardrobe malfunction. I remember one year, Sandy Brooks, who was sitting on the front row, had on the exact same long "Miss America" dress that I was wearing! We both laughed about it, joking that we had great taste. But I felt my fans wanted to see me in something unique. That's the pressure of the awards shows.

Dick Clark was a stickler for promptness! He also liked the show to run on time without a glitch. When he said, "Tighten it up," it was my responsibility as host to talk fast and to get the next act introduced. When he'd say, "Stretch," *that* was a problem for me. One year he said, "Go out and just talk to them." Now, if you know me, I'm pretty good at talking, but when Dick put me on the spot, my mind went blank. Finally Dick came out and helped me, a moment I fondly remember.

The ACMs are like a family reunion for me, a chance to visit with my buddies, whom I rarely get to see (unless we happen to be touring together). I especially love the ACM Awards when they're in Las Vegas. No one goes home after the show, and we're all in the same hotel having a fun time together. I'd tell you more, but you know the saying, what happens in Vegas, stays in Vegas. As the ACM Awards move to Dallas to celebrate the show's fiftieth anniversary, I have no doubt there will be more amazing memories in store for us.

The ACM Awards have helped push my career forward, and it's done the same for thousands of other country musicians, allowing us to share our latest singles, our albums, and our careers in front of the millions of fans watching. I hope you enjoy this look back over an amazing fifty years of great country music moments!

—REBA McENTIRE

P. 2: *Tim McGraw, 2009.*
Pp. 3–4: *The Band Perry, 2014.*
P. 5: *Taylor Swift, 2009.*
LEFT: *Reba hosting, 2009.*

INTRODUCTION

The first time I covered the Academy of Country Music Awards was in 1998, only a couple of years into my first Nashville reporting job for *TNN Country News*. I was twenty-nine years old—young and green—but even I could immediately see there was something special going on. It was the year Kenny Chesney won his first ACM award for Top New Male Vocalist—the first

award he had won in his career—and I vividly remember interviewing him right after he walked offstage with his "hat" trophy. He had brought his mom, Karen, with him, and the smile on his face said it all. He was on his way. That trophy in his hand was the first big payoff for countless late nights, low-paying gigs, and closed doors. It was the first of many accolades to come for that dreamer from east Tennessee. Standing in the crowded backstage area just outside the Universal Amphitheatre under the LA stars, Kenny's dreams were coming true that night. And it was a beautiful thing to witness.

The Academy of Country Music Awards have made dreams come true for fifty years now, for both the rising country star climbing onto the stage to accept an ACM trophy and the die-hard country fan watching at home on the living room floor. It's been that way since the Academy's four feisty founders—country-and-western performer Tommy Wiggins, songwriter Eddie Miller, and club owners Mickey and Chris Christensen—decided it was time to shine a spotlight on the hardworking musicians entertaining on the Southern California circuit. At that first "awards banquet" in 1963 at the Red Barrel Niteclub in Hawaiian Gardens, CA—with a guitar-shaped cake and buffet dinner—the movers and shakers who were giving life to the Bakersfield Sound and California country came together and created something lasting. That's why to this day the Academy of Country Music is based in Los Angeles instead of Nashville—staying true to its Southern California roots and the notion that great country music is a sound and a feeling that comes from the heart, not from a location on a map.

For more than five decades, we've seen country grow from the music heard echoing down the backroads of America into the most popular genre of music around the world. There are more country radio stations in the United States

today than any other genre—including top-rated stations in the two largest media markets in the nation: New York and Los Angeles. As country music has prospered, the Academy has also grown from a small, regional organization into a national powerhouse. Its board of directors boasts the brightest minds and biggest names in the industry, always looking for that next great way to showcase country music artists and the music they make to the world. The ACM Awards, "Country Music's Party of the Year®," is now seen by millions of viewers annually on CBS. It's amazing to look through the years and see the unbelievable artists who have graced the ACM Awards stage. From hot newcomers to Hollywood stars to country music legends, they've all had a part in making ACM history, and you'll meet them here in these pages. As editor of the Academy's magazine, *ACM Tempo*, for the last seven years, it's been great fun to dive into the photo archives. You never know who or what you'll find in there. We've gathered some of our favorites for you and talked to some of your favorite artists so you'll feel as though you were there—onstage and backstage. It's a privilege to tell their stories. A sincere thank-you to Reba, Marty Stuart, Loretta Lynn, Randy Owen, Garth Brooks, George Strait, Luke Bryan, and Blake Shelton for sharing their thoughts and personal ACM memories with us. This is a tribute to all the artists, producers, writers, musicians, stagehands, Academy board members, and ACM staffers who've helped build the ACM Awards over its fifty years.

And to Tommy, Mickey, and all those SoCal rebels who so long ago set out to make their mark on the music they loved, we fellow dreamers thank you for your foresight and courage—and for helping make our dreams, whatever they may be, come to fruition, too.

—LISA LEE, 2014

Pp. 10–11: *Taylor Swift, Sugarland, Rascal Flatts, Brooks & Dunn, and Carrie Underwood open the show, 2009.*
OPPOSITE: *Eric Church, 2014.*

1960s

1960s

Tommy Wiggins considered himself a lucky man. Relocating from his native Arizona to Southern California, the country-and-western performer found a welcoming and vibrant country music scene in the early 1960s that stretched all the way from Bakersfield to San Diego. Different from the smooth and popular "Nashville Sound" records coming out of Music City

from revered artists like Patsy Cline, Ray Price, and Jim Reeves, California country was more raw, rough, and urgent. Songs like the Joe and Rose Lee Maphis classic "Dim Lights, Thick Smoke (And Loud, Loud Music)" captured a world where long days in the fields rolled into raucous Saturday nights when the beer flowed and the bands were thumping.

The struggling farmers who moved west from states like Arkansas, Oklahoma, and Texas during the Dust Bowl migration of the 1930s, and then, later, to work in the West Coast shipyards during World War II, had brought their music with them, easing their longing for home and their new hardscrabble Southern California realities with the sounds they knew and loved. Bakersfield in particular proved a fertile ground for artists like Merle Haggard and Buck Owens to spring up.

Haggard and Owens had migrated west with their families to find a better way of life and happened to land at the epicenter of a musical revolution. "The Bakersfield Sound" was blossoming through a thriving local music scene—including

Fuzzy Owen and Lewis Talley's local label, Talley Records, and the Blackboard and the Lucky Spot, both lively clubs where musicians like Tommy Collins, Wynn Stewart, Ferlin Husky, Ralph Mooney, and Billy Mize were local stars with styles all their own. Leo Fender's hard-body electric guitars, created in Fullerton, California, and Semie Moseley's double-neck Mosrite guitars, built in Bakersfield, gave these eager players brand-new tools to craft an exciting sound that welded honky-tonk country to elements of western swing, blues, and jazz.

"A lot of things happened at the same time," Haggard explained of the Bakersfield scene. "They started making Telecaster guitars that were just made to order for playing in a bar. If you got in a fight you could use them as a baseball bat. Television was new, and local television was a big deal back then. It was like AM radio. I think the Grand Ole Opry music was more closely associated with church, and California was a little more with the barroom. Most of that,

Pp. 14–15: *George Lindsey and Billy Mize, 1968.*
ABOVE: *The Red Barrel Niteclub, the site of the first So-Cal country music awards banquet, circa 1963.*
OPPOSITE: *Tommy Wiggins in an early publicity photo.*

we'll call it 'barroom' attitude, came about in the oil fields of California and Texas and Oklahoma."

Regional TV shows like *Cousin Herb's Trading Post* and *Town Hall Party*, along with West Coast radio stations KUZZ Bakersfield, KFOX Long Beach, KWOW Pomona, KBBQ Burbank, KGBS Los Angeles, and KSON San Diego broadcasted country music to Los Angeles County and beyond. Prolific producer Ken Nelson and multi-talented A & R man Cliffie Stone turned Hollywood's legendary Capitol Records into a haven for emerging country music talent, recording Merle Travis, Jean Shepard, and Hank Thompson, and, later, Owens and Haggard. After years of local gigs and session musician work, Owens put Bakersfield on the national map in 1963 with his first number one hit, "Act Naturally," a song whose cheeky sarcasm would influence even the Beatles (who recorded the song in 1965 and released it as a B-side to "Yesterday").

ABOVE: *Host Biff Collie and songwriter Eddie Miller, 1964.*
BELOW: *Glen Campbell, Janet McBride, Gene Davis, and Tommy Wiggins at the first unofficial awards banquet at the Red Barrel Niteclub in 1963.*

Haggard, who after a troubled youth spent time in San Quentin prison for a botched robbery attempt, pulled his life together and further cemented Bakersfield's growing place in country music. He played bass in Owens' band and branded them "The Buckaroos" before establishing himself as a solo performer and thoughtful songwriter. Songs like "The Bottle Let Me Down," "Swinging Doors," and "Mama Tried" reflected Haggard's own life experiences and earned him the nickname "Poet of the Common Man."

TOP: *The first official board meeting of the Academy of Country and Western Music on February 17, 1965, at the Aces Club. From left: Eddie Drake, Mike Garro, Tommy Wiggins, Fuzzy Owen, Billy Mize, Carl West, Cliff Crofford, Gene Davis, Gordon Calcote, and Jim Olson.*
ABOVE: *Mickey (center) and Chris Christensen (right).*

THE BIG IDEA

It was in that energized Southern California world that Wiggins landed work on the bandstands of the Blackboard and Pomona's Aces Club. He was glad to have the gigs and discovered a family of kindred spirits in the performers who worked the SoCal circuit—a seemingly endless list of rooms including the Crow's Nest in Oxnard, the Ranch in El Monte, the Hitching Post in Gardena, the Foothill Club in Long Beach, and the Palomino in North Hollywood. Moonlighting as a golf pro at LA's Griffith Park, Tommy often found himself tooling around the course in the daylight hours with his fellow performers.

It was after a spirited round at Los Alameda Golf Course with songwriter and publisher Eddie Miller ("Release Me") and then up-and-coming session musician and singer Glen Campbell that the idea came for a West Coast country music awards presentation. They pondered the thought over nineteenth-hole drinks at their regular haunt, the Red Barrel Nightclub, in Hawaiian Gardens and found a supporter in owner Mickey Christensen and her husband, Chris. Mickey was a spitfire and one of the few women in the state

"I don't think Nashville knew about what was happening here in California, and there was a need for the Academy."

—MERLE HAGGARD

of California who could legally pour liquor. The Christensens offered their club as the venue, and Wiggins decided to sponsor the event through his radio publication, *D.J.'s Digest*.

"We wanted to make people aware and also reward those talented people in the Southern California area who were being ignored by Nashville with the recognition that they deserved," Wiggins explained. "We had some of the best entertainers in the country-and-western music field at that time. If you went to Nashville and you could stick it out for five years, then you had a chance of sticking around, but most of the people couldn't afford to spend five years of their life to make it. We wanted to do something with the power that we were acquiring by coming together as a group. It was a pretty powerful entity."

Miller went to work organizing the event, entertainer Tex Williams signed on as the emcee, and the first "D.J.'s Digest Awards" were handed out at the Red Barrel Niteclub on November 18, 1963. Despite its proximity to Hollywood, the original awards banquet was a low-key and down-home affair.

"I said, 'I'll furnish the club, the entertainment, the band, and cater the food,' which was a joke because it was potluck," Mickey Christensen later recalled in a 2009 interview. "We put four-by-eight boards on the pool tables and had a big layout of food. It was more of a party, and it was great fun."

The buzz on the event was so good that a second awards banquet was held at the Red Barrel on November 30, 1964, this time sponsored by Jim Olson's *V.I.P. Club Guide* and dubbed the "Country Music Awards of Southern California." Supporting the show in those early years was a who's who from the Southern California music scene—Campbell, country DJs Biff Collie and Carl "Squeakin' Deacon" Moore, Western movie star Eddie Dean, *Cal's Corral* host Sammy

BELOW: *Merle Haggard was recognized as Male Star of the Year at the 1964 Southern California Country Music Awards. With Merle are KFOX's Gordon Calcote, fellow winner Wynn Stewart, and master of ceremonies Biff Collie.*

LEFT: *Jeannie Seely accepts "Up & Coming Female Vocalist" in 1964.*
BELOW: *An early Academy newsletter.*

Masters, and *Trading Post Show* host and musician Billy Mize. Among the winners the first two years were Buck Owens, who was honored for "Loyalty to Country Music on the West Coast" and Merle Haggard, who was recognized as "Male Star of the Year," a year before he would record his debut album *Strangers* at the legendary Capitol Records.

"I don't think Nashville knew about what was happening here in California, and there was a need for the Academy," Haggard said. "The Academy of Country Music, I think, noticed the obvious need for what they had to give and what they could offer in promotion. So, it was a good thing for everybody, and it came about at a time when there was a lot to show people. There was a lot going on here. Buck Owens was in the beginning, and Ferlin Husky and Tommy Collins and a lot of other artists that were maybe lesser artists, but at the same time Bob Wills was touring this part of the country and he was big. It was something to see, and I'm glad I got to see it."

Also honored was future Grand Ole Opry star Jeannie Seely, who shared the Up & Coming Female Vocalist award with "yodeling queen" Janet McBride and singer Betty Foster.

"I remember how exciting it was that everybody was all together in one place because we didn't have that," Seely said. "I must tell this, and Merle will forgive me I know, but one of the main things I remember [is that] when they told me that Merle Haggard was nominated as most promising male artist and that we would be seated and interviewed together, I was scared to

ACADEMY OF COUNTRY AND WESTERN MUSIC

2nd Annual Country & Western Awards

This is the second year in which the Academy of Country and Western Music has made awards and the jam-packed dinner at the Beverly Hilton on March 6th attests to the solid stature of country music in general.

Most of the greats of country music were there. Lorne Greene was host-narrator and among award presenters were Andy Devine, Pat Buttram, Chill Wills, Eddie Albert, Judy Lynn, Nick Adams, Brenda Scott, Edgar Buchanan and Donna Douglas.

Dean Martin was hailed as Country and Western "Man of the Year," with Academy President Tex Williams making the presentation. Winners included Bob Morris, Bill Mize, Merle Haggard, Jimmy Bryant, Tom Brumley, Ralph Monney, Jerry Wiggins, Billy Armstrong, Billy Liebert, and Bonnie Guitar.

Among the entertaining groups were Roger Miller, Tex Ritter, Sons of the Pioneers, Ray Price and Tex Williams.

A 26-member band of Local 47's finest, under the baton of Carl Cotner, played the background and theme music for the evening.

ABOVE: Carl Cotner's Orchestra and personalities at the award dinner; THREE PICTURES ON RIGHT: Top, Edgar Buchanan, Andy Devine, Pat Buttram and Chill Wills . . . they presented awards; Center, Tex Williams and an academy official greet Mayor Yorty and John Tranchitella; Bottom: The Sons of the Pioneers.

up + Coming Female Vocalists *Betty Foster* *Janet McBride* *Jeannie Seely* *1964*

1964 VIP Awards

TOP: *Biff Collie, Betty Foster, Janet McBride, and Jeannie Seely, 1964.*
ABOVE: *Winners at the 1964 Country Music Awards of Southern California.*
OPPOSITE: *Janet McBride accepts "Female Vocalist" from emcee Tex Williams, 1963.*

"It was booming in Southern California, and I just happened to step in at the perfect time."
—JANET McBRIDE

death because I had heard that Merle had been in prison. I didn't know what for and all I knew was that my mama said, 'Stay away from those bad folks!' So, I was a little bit scared of Merle Haggard! I have to say, I'm over it now."

McBride, who also won Female Vocalist at the banquet in '63, explained that the awards came just in time to give a little push to the working musicians who were plugging away down the California coast.

"Southern California was alive. The DJs were coming alive. It was booming in Southern California, and I just happened to step in at a perfect time," McBride said from her current home in Forney, Texas. (She would go on to teach yodeling to countless young Texas singers, including LeAnn Rimes and Kacey Musgraves.) "I don't think any of the recognition happened until Buck Owens blew the lid off of the world. Even Glen [Campbell] wasn't getting the recognition that he would later get in those days. Nobody was getting any recognition out of Nashville, and that, of course, was it. That was where the big stuff was happening, and we all wanted to be a part of it. So I think it was just an underlying boiling pit of people who wanted some recognition. So Tommy said, 'Let's do it. Let's have some recognition. Let's have some awards.'"

HOSTS & LOCATIONS

1966 · Lorne Green

THE HOLLYWOOD PALLADIUM, HOLLYWOOD, CA

1967 · Lorne Green

THE BEVERLY HILTON HOTEL, LOS ANGELES, CA

1968 · Pat Buttram

THE CENTURY PLAZA HOTEL, LOS ANGELES, CA

1969 · Dick Clark

THE HOLLYWOOD PALLADIUM, HOLLYWOOD, CA

Dick Clark, Billy Mize, Joanie Somers, Biff Collie, and Buck Owens at the ACWM Awards, 1966.

THE EARLY YEARS

The first two "awards banquets" were so success-ful that a group of heavyweights on the West Coast country scene—including Wiggins, Mize, Collie, Stone, KFOX manager Dick Schofield, and tailor Nudie Cohn, among others—got together to create a formal organization to help promote country music in the Western states. After pre-liminary talks in 1964, the first official meeting was documented on February 17, 1965, at the Aces Club. Through the help of early supporter Eddie Dean, movie star Gene Autry offered his support, giving the fledgling Academy of Country and Western Music—as it was now called—a free meeting space for a year in his own Continental Hotel on Sunset Boulevard (which would later be sold and become known as the infamous "Riot House," frequented in the 1970s by rock stars like the Rolling Stones, The Who, and Led Zeppelin, and the site of legendary rock-n-roll debauchery). The early board of directors—which included songwriter Mae Boren Axton and radio personal-ity Bob Kingsley—elected Williams as its first pres-ident and decided to take the show to Hollywood, staging the first official Academy of Country and Western Music Awards on February 28, 1966, at

the Hollywood Palladium to honor the best music of 1965. (In Nashville, the Country Music Asso-ciation had already formed in 1958 as the first country music trade organization but had yet to stage its own awards show.)

Those first shows were an interesting cock-tail of country-and-western singers and Hol-lywood stars like Lorne Greene; Don Knotts; George "Goober" Lindsey; Della Reese; *The Beverly Hillbillies'* stars Irene Ryan, Donna Douglas, and Buddy Ebsen; and TV and radio personality Dick Clark—a unique mix that

TOP: Bonanza's *Lorne Greene handled hosting duties for the 2nd Academy of Country and Western Music Awards on March 7, 1967 at the Beverly Hilton Hotel.*
ABOVE: *Bakersfield radio station KUZZ's 1966 newsletter.*

would become the show's trademark. Buck Owens was named Top Male Vocalist, and Bonnie Owens was named Top Female Vocalist. Haggard was named Most Promising Male Vocalist while he and Bonnie also won Best Vocal Group. Other winners for 1965 included Roger Miller as Songwriter of the Year, Capitol's Ken Nelson as Producer/A&R Man, and North Hollywood's Palomino Club as Outstanding Country Music Club.

As the decade came to a close, the Academy named Arizona native Marty Robbins its first Artist of the Decade. Robbins learned to play the guitar during World War II and then made his way to Nashville with the help of Grand Ole Opry star Little Jimmy Dickens. After charting both pop and country hits in the 1950s that showcased his versatility as a vocalist, Robbins released his platinum-selling album *Gunfighter Ballads and Trail Songs* and now-classic country hits like "El Paso" and "Don't Worry." His sense of humor and larger-than-life personality made him a popular figure from coast to coast.

Nº: 320

Academy of Country & Western Music

Third Annual Awards Dinner

Monday, March 4, 1968

in the

Los Angeles Ballroom

Century Plaza Hotel - Century City

Cocktails 6:30 p.m.   Dinner 8 p.m.

Dinner $15.00   Black Tie Optional   Table No. 23

OPPOSITE CLOCKWISE: *Marty Robbins; Glen Campbell, Cathie Taylor, Dinah Shore, and Jim Nabors, 1969; Bob Kingsley with his parents, Don and Lillian Kingsley, 1968; Ray Price performs, 1967.*

ARTIST OF THE DECADE
MARTY ROBBINS

I recently saw a bumper sticker in Los Angeles that read, "Welcome to LA, pick a decade and fit in." If I had to choose any particular place and time within the existence of country music, unquestionably Southern California in the 1960s would be my idea of our Camelot moment. Think of Fender guitars; the sound of Ralph Mooney's steel guitar; living in Toluca Lake; being kissed by the scent of jasmine while riding down Lankershim Boulevard in a highly chromed, jet-black Cadillac convertible; roses year 'round; a trip to Nudie's Rodeo Tailors; honky-tonkin' at the Palomino; the lovely California girls; having breakfast at the Sportsmen's in the morning with Gene Autry, Monte Hale, Pat Buttram, and their cowboy pals; palm trees; the ocean; the sound of the Bakersfield boys coming through the speakers at Capitol Records; hanging out with Hugh Cherry, Biff Collie, Cliffie Stone; talking songwriting, guitars, and such with Merle Travis; visiting Ed Bohlin's Saddle Shop in Hollywood; feeling time stand still the first moment "Wichita Lineman" came on the radio in the Golden State; and being touched by the magic of the late afternoon Pacific light. There's nothing like it anywhere else on earth. It's no wonder California country music was so special. It was a reflection of Heaven on earth. The music was mighty, and it lives on with an eternal smile. So does the memory and the music of the Academy of Country Music's Artist of the Decade of the 1960s, Marty Robbins. He was a continental troubadour, a man for the ages, a cat among cats.

In the 1920s, the Father of Country Music, Jimmie Rodgers, gave us the blueprint to our musical existence by way of the subject matter in his songs. Jimmie wrote songs that explored themes we've all come to know well. His lyrics spoke of rambling, gambling, cheating, mistreating, drinking, sinning, cowboying, outlawing, and hoboing. He sang about the blues, blue trains, lonesome railroads, jailhouses, rogues, Mother, home, the land, love, hard luck, and hard times, about being weary, tired, lonely and sad, about the mysteries of Heaven, Hell, planet Earth, and all points in between. These themes fueled the imagination and found their mark in the heart of an Arizona kid named Marty Robbins. He took the creative licenses that Jimmie Rodgers offered and, over time, built upon them, creating his own vast body of work. In a voice that could be described as otherworldly, Marty Robbins sang his brand of country music like no one before or since.

Marty Robbins was a musical adventurer who possessed a fearless creative spirit. He sang songs of love and romance. He cast his spell as he carried us away on his voice to the Hawaiian Islands. He made us want to dance, sang us the blues, sang us the stories of days gone by as well as songs of better days yet to come. "Devil Woman," "You Gave Me a Mountain," and "My Woman, My Woman, My Wife" are always mentioned as his finest. However it is his Gunfighter Ballads and Trail Songs project, which included the song "El Paso," that seems to stand as his Arc de Triomphe. It

never goes away. Like the man himself, Gunfighter Ballads and Trail Songs continues to be a force for the ages.

Merle Haggard and I once talked about Marty Robbins and his impact on our culture. Merle's observation was, "The world is filled with imitators, but I've yet to meet the man who could pull Marty Robbins' train. It's too deep in there. It's the pure sound of his voice that was so much of his power, and that can never be duplicated."

One of the people that Marty Robbins touched with his beautiful voice was my mother, Hilda Stuart. Mama loved Marty's singing enough to name me after him. I met him for the first time backstage at the Grand Ole Opry in 1972. I had just joined Lester Flatt's band. He came into our dressing room to tell me that he had heard me playing the mandolin on the radio on the way to the Opry. He paid me some nice compliments. I thanked him and told him that I'd always wanted to meet him because my mother loved his singing to the extent of naming me after him when I was born. He said, "No kidding? Your mother is a wise woman. As you get older, you'll find that you are named after one of the greatest human beings to ever walk the earth." And then he high-fived me. Everyone broke out laughing and Lester ran him out of the dressing room. He left us smiling.

Artist of the decade for the 1960s, sure, or any other one for that matter. Here's to Marty Robbins and California.

WITH LOVE, MARTY STUART

OPPOSITE: *Artist of the Decade Marty Robbins preforms.*
ABOVE: *Marty Robbins and Waylon Jennings, 1969.*

In 1968, a U.S. Air Force disc jockey named Bill Boyd and his wife, Fran, first became involved with the Academy. Boyd, a native of Jackson, Tennessee, whose childhood friend was Carl Perkins, had hosted a radio show in Germany and had nurtured relationships with the country artists who came through the base. A visit from Academy President Tex Williams proved prophetic.

"Tex came over and did his tour, and he was talking about this organization, the Academy of Country and Western Music, and I said, 'Oh, that sounds interesting. I'd like to see what that is all about,'" remembers Fran Boyd. "Later Tex gave Bill an Academy membership card and said, 'Now you're a member of the Academy and I can nominate you for the board of directors.'"

When the Air Force relocated the Boyds to Los Angeles, both Bill and Fran became active with the new organization—an association that would last more than thirty years. Bill was elected to the board of directors and later served as president and talent producer for the awards show. Fran became the organization's first paid employee, taking over secretary duties from volunteer Bettie Azevedo.

"They paid me enough to get my cleaning done and get the babysitter paid," Fran recalled with a chuckle.

In 1969, the Academy landed its first office in Hollywood near Crossroads of the World. After seven years, the Academy of Country and Western Music Awards was gaining momentum and setting the stage for a more national presence to come in the 1970s.

"Originally, the Academy was only going to recognize country music from Nevada west," said Mize, who was honored at the 1964 show for "Contribution to Country Music Thru Television" and would go on to win four more awards from the organization. "But after several meetings, we realized we couldn't limit our recognition. We had to give all country music artists the recognition they deserved."

"Originally, the Academy was only going to recognize country music from Nevada west, but we realized we couldn't limit our recognition."
—BILLY MIZE

By decade's end, the little "awards banquet" that started at the Red Barrel in 1963 had become the fan to the flames ignited by the talented artists on the West Coast, causing Nashville and the rest of the country to take notice of the musicians and the music that would inspire generations to come.

OPPOSITE TOP: *Bill Boyd, left, in the early days of his role as a talent executive for the Academy at the 1969 show at the Hollywood Palladium with Musical Director Billy Liebert.*
OPPOSITE BOTTOM LEFT: *California native and early Academy supporter Cliffie Stone, center, with Red Wooten and Earl Ball in 1969. After Stone's death in January 1998, the board of directors renamed a special award the "Cliffie Stone Pioneer Award."*
OPPOSITE BOTTOM RIGHT: *TV Personality of the Year Glen Campbell (right) with Man of the year Tom Smothers, 1969.*
ABOVE: *Merle Haggard and Bonnie Owens accept the Top Duo trophy in 1968, with presenters Peter Breck and Richard Long.*

1970s

1970s

F rom the outside, 1970s country seemed to fall into two categories—the smooth "countrypolitan" sound of Glen Campbell and Charlie Rich, and the grittier "outlaw" movement of Willie Nelson and Waylon Jennings. While songs like Campbell's "Rhinestone Cowboy" found new fans on the pop charts, Willie and Waylon's *Wanted! The Outlaws* album with Jessi Colter and

Tompall Glaser struck a deep chord with a growing group of country rockers, becoming the first country album to sell more than one million copies. *Rolling Stone* even put Nelson on the cover in 1978, an issue in which journalist Chet Flippo wrote that Willie was challenging the very notion of "what is and is not country music." If countrypolitan was the boy you took home to meet your parents (safe and respectable), outlaw country was the boy you snuck out your window to meet after midnight (dangerous and unpredictable).

No matter which side of the "what is and is not country music" debate fans found themselves on, one thing was undeniable—country was on its way to becoming more mainstream.

Loretta Lynn embodied this appeal to both the country and the commercial. With hit songs like "Coal Miner's Daughter," Lynn reached beyond the country core, and she was a live wire whose genuine personality fascinated the general public. Put her in front of a microphone,

P. 32: *Crystal Gayle performs, 1977.*
TOP: *Charlie Rich and Roy Clark at the 9th Annual ACM Awards on March 25, 1974.*
ABOVE: *Entertainer of the Year Loretta Lynn visits with Roy Rogers and Dale Evans at the 1976 ACM Awards.*
OPPOSITE: *Johnny Rodriguez, Loretta Lynn, Freddie Hart, and Tanya Tucker backstage, 1973.*

ABOVE: *Loretta Lynn performs, 1973.*
RIGHT: *Loretta and ACM Pioneer Award winner Gene Autry backstage, 1973.*

and, if she wasn't singing, you never really knew what she was going to say. That pure down-home charm made her a darling among country music fans as well, and it made for great TV.

"Tonight I won't be singing 'The Pill' because they wouldn't let me," Loretta ad-libbed on the 1975 ACM Awards during her acceptance speech for Top Female Vocalist of the Year. But she didn't let the network censors slow her down, instead throwing an additional punch during a later performance of her hit "You Ain't Woman Enough (To Take My Man)."

"Don't worry, you can't take my man now, I've got the pill," she deadpanned right to the TV cameras.

Loretta embodied the long-standing creed of country music—sing the truth about what you know—and her sassy personality was right at home among the country stars who graced the ACM Awards stage during the 1970s.

THE ACMs GO LIVE

It was during the '70s that the ACMs began to morph from the West Coast–centered awards banquets of the 1960s into a bona fide national TV franchise. Moving to the John Wayne Theater at Knott's Berry Farm in 1972, the show was broadcast in syndication for the first time through Metromedia. Longtime radio host and TV producer Gene Weed came on to produce the show with his brother, Ron Weed, through their production company Film Factory. They approached ABC network executives in 1973 about airing the show nationally. After a year of negotiations, during which Gene said he had to convince the network brass that country

ABOVE: *ACM "Trophy Girls," 1972.*
LEFT: *Fran Boyd and Gene Weed backstage at Knott's Berry Farm, 1972.*

ABOVE: *Lynn Anderson at rehearsals, 1972.*
TOP RIGHT: *Comedy Act of the Year Roy Clark (left) with George Lindsey, 1972.*
RIGHT: *Tom T. Hall and Donna Fargo, 1973.*
OPPOSITE: *Kenny Rogers and the First Edition perform "Reuben James" on the 1972 ACM Awards.*

fans would stay up late enough to watch the show in an 11:30 P.M. time slot, ABC agreed. The show, now called the Academy of Country Music Awards (the organization dropped the "Western" from its name after some heated debate among the board of directors), was taped live and aired coast-to-coast three days later on March 28, 1974.

"It captured one of the highest ratings of any show ever aired in that time slot, despite the fact that a highly publicized 'streaker' made a flash appearance on the Carson show that same

"ABC was delighted, the in-house audience had a ball, and the television audience was introduced to the Academy of Country Music."
—PRODUCER GENE WEED

night," Weed would recount in a later interview. "ABC was delighted, the in-house audience had a ball, and the television audience was introduced to the Academy of Country Music."

The ACM Awards were riding a wave of country-themed programming that had started in 1969 with the debuts of *The Johnny Cash Show*, *The Glen Campbell Goodtime Hour* (each won their hosts ACM trophies for Television Personality of the Year), and *Hee-Haw*, which brought

both country music and humor to the masses through network television. Although many country- or rural-themed shows were dropped in what is known as the networks' "rural purge" of 1971 (which canceled long-running popular shows that were seen as skewing to older, more rural viewers), somehow Weed was able to help the ACM Awards escape a similar fate.

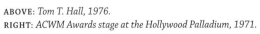
ABOVE: *Tom T. Hall, 1976.*
RIGHT: *ACWM Awards stage at the Hollywood Palladium, 1971.*

The show's writers—which in the early days included Southern California disc jockey Hugh Cherry and up-and-coming actor Alan Thicke (who would go on to fame in the '80s starring in the hit sitcom *Growing Pains*)—tried hard to bridge the gap between down-home and uptown. Thicke worked as a writer for a decade before moving in front of the camera as an actor, and he had written network TV specials for country acts Johnny Cash, Glen Campbell, Mac Davis, and his fellow Canadian Anne Murray. He said the Hollywood setting for the ACMs gave him some leeway in the script.

"I remember one specific joke I wrote that would be borderline politically incorrect now," Thicke said. "I needed to come up with something for us to introduce Barbi Benton, the *Playboy* centerfold who dabbled in country music. If the show were emanating from Nashville that year, she probably wouldn't have made the cut. The very fact that it was in Hollywood sort of opened the tent I think a little wider. So, Roger Miller had to introduce her, and I wrote a joke that was something like 'and here's a gal with a great future. . . . and not a bad behind.' Got a good laugh. It was a good joke."

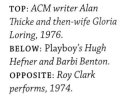

TOP: *ACM writer Alan Thicke and then-wife Gloria Loring, 1976.*
BELOW: Playboy's *Hugh Hefner and Barbi Benton.*
OPPOSITE: *Roy Clark performs, 1974.*

The first performer on the syndicated Academy show was *Hee-Haw* star Roy Clark, who took the stage to play "Alabama Jubilee" after the announcer opened the show with the line "We're here to give the country beat its own delicious flavor, the flavor of sweet country ham sautéed in champagne." Producers took advantage of their proximity to Hollywood, booking a seemingly endless parade of star presenters from the hottest TV shows of the day—from *M*A*S*H*'s Gary Burghoff to *Happy Days'* Anson Williams and Donny Most. Even the world's most famous bachelor, *Playboy* founder Hugh Hefner, attended the show in support of his then-girlfriend and ACM Awards presenter Benton.

HOSTS & LOCATIONS

1970 · Buddy Ebsen

THE HOLLYWOOD PALLADIUM, HOLLYWOOD, CA

1971 · Dick Clark

THE HOLLYWOOD PALLADIUM, HOLLYWOOD, CA

1972 · Dick Clark

KNOTT'S BERRY FARM, BUENA PARK, CA

1973 · Dick Clark

KNOTT'S BERRY FARM, BUENA PARK, CA

1974 · Roger Miller & Charlie Rich

KNOTT'S BERRY FARM, BUENA PARK, CA

1975 · Roger Miller & Loretta Lynn

KNOTT'S BERRY FARM, BUENA PARK, CA

1976 · Marty Robbins

THE HOLLYWOOD PALLADIUM, HOLLYWOOD, CA

1977 · Pat Boone, Patti Page & Jerry Reed

SHRINE AUDITORIUM, HOLLYWOOD, CA

1978 · Donna Fargo, Kenny Rogers
& Barbara Mandrell

SHRINE AUDITORIUM, HOLLYWOOD, CA

1979 · Roy Clark, Barbara Mandrell
& Dennis Weaver

THE HOLLYWOOD PALLADIUM, HOLLYWOOD, CA

OPPOSITE: *Dick Clark, 1971.*

TOP: *Charley Pride and Merle Haggard at The Hollywood Palladium, 1971.*
ABOVE: *ACM Award winners Don Williams and Freddy Fender backstage, 1979.*
OPPOSITE: *Roger Miller hosts, 1974.*

Roger Miller, who hosted the 1974 broadcast, addressed the Hollywood mix and country's growing popularity.

"It wasn't too many years ago we country fans were considered a small minority, a smattering of boot-wearing, foot-stomping folks who couldn't spell acceptance, much less say it," Miller said to the national TV audience. "But me and Jimmy Dean, Glen Campbell, Bobbie Gentry, Ray Price, Johnny Cash, and some other notable folks thought there was a better way and started to break down some barriers and open some doors to radio, television, movies, and Las Vegas, and suddenly, country was everybody's music."

The success of Charley Pride was a sign that some of the doors were opening. One of the first African American performers in country music, Pride was welcomed by the Academy members, who nominated him for Entertainer of the Year three times during the 1970s. He was a popular show host as well, helping guide the live broadcast in 1980 with cohosts Loretta Lynn and actor Claude Akins.

"[Loretta] was one of my biggest supporters," Pride said. "She kissed me on the TV and that was something I don't think had ever been done too much. Somebody said something to her about it and she said, 'I'll kiss him again.' That's the way she felt about it."

Glimpses of diversity were also evident in Mexican American artists Johnny Rodriguez and Freddy Fender, who were named Most Promising Male Vocalist by Academy voters in 1972 and 1975, respectively.

The involvement of popular TV icon and *American Bandstand* host Dick Clark as master of ceremonies in 1971, 1972, and 1973 would lend clout to the fledgling franchise. His influence would really be felt in 1979, when Clark put his production company behind the show and signed on as executive producer. The Academy of Country Music Awards moved from ABC to NBC and went from a live-to-tape program to a full-on live production. "We went from 'sleepy time' on ABC to 'prime time' on NBC," Gene Weed later joked.

ABOVE: *Teenager Tanya Tucker sings "Delta Dawn," 1973.*
ABOVE RIGHT: *ACM Award winner Conway Twitty performs, February 26th, 1973.*

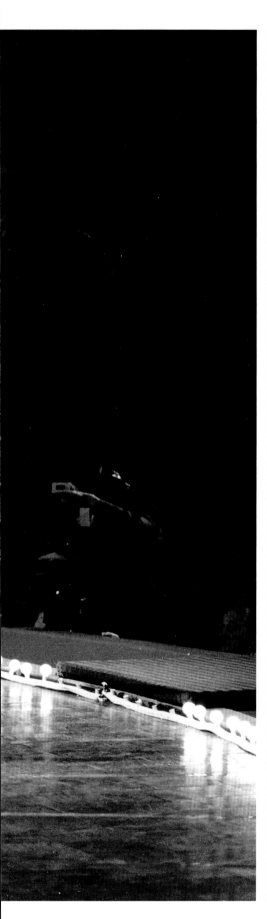

TOP: *Kenny Rogers (left) and Dick Clark (right) with "Easy Lovin'" singer Freddie Hart, 1972.*
ABOVE: Roots *stars Levar Burton and Ren Woods present an award in 1977.*
OPPOSITE TOP: *Pee Wee King (left) and Patsy Montana (right) with ACM Pioneer Award winner Tennessee Ernie Ford, 1975.*
OPPOSITE BOTTOM: *Dottie West presents with* Starsky & Hutch *star David Soul, 1978.*

"I think probably the pitch when Dick and Gene brought it to the networks was 'This is where country and Hollywood meet,' because they were all pretty authentic country people that you would think were country fans or came from the South, but they were Hollywood stars as well," explained Barry Adelman, who worked as a writer for dick clark productions and would eventually join the Academy show as a writer and producer.

Roy Clark, Barbara Mandrell, and Dennis Weaver hosted the first live broadcast, which featured a show opener with some help from the Dallas Cowboy Cheerleaders. "It was more produced than *Gone with the Wind*," Roy Clark remarked about the intricate number. These early ACM shows were patterned after the popular variety shows of the day—lots of stars, music, and country humor.

"The ACMs has always been a great barometer of what country music is and has been and will

Pee Wee King   Ernie Ford   Patsy Montana

be," said Joe Bonsall of the Oak Ridge Boys, who won their first industry trophy at the 1979 ACM Awards. "When you're a young act and you've been struggling and struggling and things start happening for you, and then you win an award at this show, man that's just a big deal."

"The ACMs has always been a great barometer of what country music is and has been and will be."
—JOE BONSALL OF
THE OAK RIDGE BOYS

Longtime Academy of Country Music board member and officer Bill Boyd continued in his role as talent producer as the show went national, calling on his strong relationships with country artists from his Armed Forces Radio days. A-list country performers Roger Miller, Marty Robbins, Kenny Rogers, Donna Fargo, and Dottie West hosted and performed on the show through the decade as it bounced from homes at the Hollywood Palladium, the Shrine Auditorium, and Knott's Berry Farm.

RIGHT: *ACM Award–winner Crystal Gayle rehearses at the Shrine Auditorium, 1977.* BELOW: *Oak Ridge Boys perform, 1979.* OPPOSITE: *Early ACM newsletter.*

Academy of Country Music

Vol. VIII No. 4 April, 1979   THE CHRONICLE OF COUNTRY MUSIC   HOLLYWOOD, CALIFORNIA

'79 AWARDS SHOW — BIGGEST EVER

By Gene Weed
ACM Show Producer

By now, I hope, you have all heard that the Academy's 14 annual awards presentation will be aired live over the NBC television network, Wednesday, May 2, 1979. If you haven't heard, wake

KENNY ROGERS

up or you'll miss the country music show of the year.

The show will take place at the Hollywood Palladium on Wednesday, May 2, 1979. The live television show will begin promptly at 6:00 p.m., airing live 9:00 to 11:00 p.m. Eastern time, 8:00 to 10:00 p.m. Central and Mountain time and from 9:00 to 11:00 p.m. (tape delayed)

THE OAK RIDGE BOYS

Pacific time. Those of you planning to attend the show will have to be inside the Palladium at 5:15 p.m. as the doors will close at 5:30 p.m. and the show will begin *exactly* at 6:00 p.m. Following the live television show, the Academy of

Country Music will present additional awards in the categories not included in the television show. The Academy will also hold a sit down dinner (dinner tickets are available through the Academy office at $40.00 per person, this includes a delicious New York steak dinner). Each dinner ticket purchased will be accompanied by a complimentary invitation to the television show. It will be necessary for you to show both your dinner ticket and your invitation when you arrive at the Palladium.

Due to the limited number of seats available you should make your reservations as soon as possible. Con-

LORETTA LYNN

DOTTIE WEST

tact the Academy office about your tickets *now*.

This year it will be my pleasure to co-produce the show with Al Schwartz for the Dick Clark Company. Our life-time member, Dick Clark, will be executive producer and brother Ron Weed will be associate producer. Tom Bruner, who has been our arranger-conductor for the past several years, will again wave his hickory baton in front of the orchestra.

At press time the following celebrities are committed to appear on the "Academy Awards of Country Music";

(Continued on Page 5, Column 3)

MEMBERSHIP MEETING NOTICE

FREE!! FREE!! MEMBERSHIP GETS SPECIAL TREAT FOR APRIL MEETING!! FREE!!

The April General Membership Meeting will be held April 9th at The Palomino Club in North Hollywood, at 6907 Lankershim. Our Host, Tommy Thomas, has generously offered to give us a special treat . . . every Academy member will be admitted free, AND also given a FREE BUFFET!! Guests of members will still be expected to pay the $2 admission charge and, if they wish to eat the buffet, will be charged $3. DON'T MISS THIS SPECIAL FREE ADMISSION AND BUFFET ON MONDAY, APRIL 9TH, STARTING AT 6 O'CLOCK!!!

MEMBERSHIP FEES

AS OF JUNE 1, 1977, MEMBERSHIP FEES IN THE ACADEMY OF COUNTRY MUSIC ARE AS FOLLOWS: PROFESSIONAL MEMBERSHIP $20.00 PER YEAR . . . GENERAL MEMBERSHIP $15.00 PER YEAR . . . FOR APPLICATIONS OR INFORMATION REGARDING MEMBERSHIP IN THE ACADEMY OF COUNTRY MUSIC, WRITE TO ACM, P.O. BOX 508, HOLLYWOOD, CA. 90028 OR TELEPHONE AREA CODE (213) 462-2351.

OPPOSITE: *Four-time ACM Award winner Charlie Rich performs, 1974.*
TOP: *Lorne Greene, Nudie Cohn, Audrey Meadows, and Robert Six, 1976.*
ABOVE: *Glen Campbell, Mac Davis, and Claude Akins, 1975.*

ABOVE: *Pat Boone, Patti Page, Mickey Gilley, and Crystal Gayle, 1977.*
RIGHT: *Entertainer of the Year Kenny Rogers, 1979.*
OPPOSITE TOP: *Loretta Lynn, Dinah Shore, and Crystal Gayle with ACM trophies, 1976.*
OPPOSITE BOTTOM: *Loretta Lynn and Conway Twitty accept Top Vocal Group, 1975.*

KEEPIN' IT COUNTRY

Although strong female performers like Tammy Wynette, Dolly Parton, and Crystal Gayle were making great strides in the male-dominated market—recording massive hit anthems like "Till I Can Make It On My Own," "I Will Always Love You," and "Don't It Make My Brown Eyes Blue"—it was the men who came to the podium to collect the most ACM Awards in the '70s, with multiple trophies going to Merle Haggard,

"It's been a good ride. I'm going to ride it right on. I ain't gonna get off this boat."
—LORETTA LYNN

Mickey Gilley, Freddie Hart, Charlie Rich, and Kenny Rogers. Still, it was Loretta Lynn who would best them all. She won five ACM trophies with her favorite duet partner, Conway Twitty—four as Top Vocal Group, as well as Album of the Year for *Feelings*. She became the first woman to win Entertainer of the Year for

1975, followed by Artist of the Decade in 1979. Loretta transcended the genre and became a mainstream national star, running the gamut from a guest-starring turn on *The Muppet Show* to being the subject of the critically acclaimed biopic *Coal Miner's Daughter* (which won actress Sissy Spacek an Academy Award). No matter how famous she became or how much pressure she was under to cross over to the pop world, Loretta's feet remained firmly planted in country music, and her successes would blow the doors open for women of the '80s and '90s to take up residence on the country charts right beside the boys.

"If you're country, you're country," Loretta said. "I thought, 'It's been a good ride, I'm going to ride it right on. I ain't gonna get off this boat.'"

LORETTA LYNN

The ACM Awards have always been my favorite awards show. I hosted a few times over the years, and I had a ball. I didn't know beans from taters about hosting, but I had a ball trying. I never could read those dern cue cards right!

You never knew who you might see backstage or in the audience. It was in Hollywood in the early years, so there were always movie and TV stars out there with all us country singers. One year I got to visit with my idol, Roy Rogers. I was in love with Roy Rogers when I was growing up. Roy Rogers was my boyfriend—he just didn't know it! One time he was sitting at a table with his wife, Dale Evans, and I walked up there and I said, "Roy, you've been my boyfriend for one hundred years." He blushed like a teenage boy. And he looked just as good as he did when he was twenty-five years old, even though he was much older. I don't know how he kept himself looking like that, but he did.

Some of my best memories of the ACMs are winning Top Vocal Group with my good buddy Conway Twitty. Conway was probably one of the greatest country singers in the business. He did not get the recognition that he deserved, as far as I'm concerned. Conway was bashful. No one would know this, but he was very, very bashful. I would do things to get him a little recognition, but it would embarrass him at the time. He would say, "Loretta, you're embarrassing me to death." When I started working with Conway, he didn't even say hello to the crowd. He would walk out on stage with his right arm in the air and the drums would start and Conway sang. He sang his hind end off. Nobody could touch him as far as I was concerned, but he would not talk. I made him sign autographs with me at night when the show was over. I said, "Conway, if you're going to be in country music, you're going to have to sign autographs. You're going to have to get out here and talk one-on-one with these fans, because if you don't, you're not going to have any fans." And it just about killed him, but he did it. He listened to everything I said. One year on the ACM Awards we won Top Vocal Group, and during our acceptance speech I teased him 'cause he wouldn't say nothing. The next year we presented an award together, and he got me back. The writers gave him a real long speech with lots of big words that were hard to get out. But he pulled it off, and it was so funny! I was tickled to death when the Academy of Country Music recognized our songs together, and he was, too.

They say I made history at the ACM Awards, and I guess I really did. In 1975, I was the first woman named Entertainer of the Year. At that point, I was the only girl who had ever been nominated for Entertainer, and I couldn't figure out why. Usually men got that. And then I got it, and I said, "Hey, more power to 'em." That was the first time that I ever got the Entertainer of the Year on any show, and I thought that was great. I just kept on working. I was the first woman who stepped out and said things that shouldn't have been said. I didn't realize that I was saying anything I shouldn't be saying; I just wrote the songs and sang them thinking, "Hey, this is life. Everybody's lived

it." But I found out different. You don't talk about some of the life you live. They hollered about my song "The Pill," and they started hollering about "One's On the Way," and I said, "Who ain't having a baby today who's my age?" I said, "I don't understand y'all taking such a hit with this because it's just everyday life, and you're living it, so it's no secret. Why not sing about it?"

No matter how much squawking anyone did, those songs hit home with the fans because they were living the exact same things I was living.

In 1979, the Academy named me its Artist of the Decade. I accepted the trophy at the 1980 ACMs with Mommy and my sister Crystal standing right beside me. The rest of my family was out in the audience, and I just remember being tickled to death. I truly couldn't believe I had done it. That was the same year that *Coal Miner's Daughter* came out, and I was on cloud nine.

I just celebrated my fiftieth anniversary in country music, and the ACM Awards are celebrating their fiftieth anniversary, too. It's very, very important that we still have this show. Back in the '70s, I think people kind of looked down on country music until they saw the Academy make such a big deal out of it on national TV. The Academy of Country Music let you be country. They let you do what you wanted to do. I found that out when I went out to LA to help them with the show. It grew into something bigger, and I watched it grow. I think we grew together.

Now country music is accepted all over the world. There's a big market for country, and I just hope the new artists don't let us down. Country is here to stay if the new artists play their cards right. While they're working hard to pave the way for a new generation of country music artists, I'm beginning to take some time off, just doing what I want to do these days. It's about time, ain't it?

—LORETTA LYNN

ACM Entertainer *of the* Year Winners

1970
MERLE HAGGARD

1971
FREDDIE HART

1972
ROY CLARK

1973
ROY CLARK

1974
MAC DAVIS

1975
LORETTA LYNN

1976
MICKEY GILLEY

1977
DOLLY PARTON

1978
KENNY ROGERS

1979
WILLIE NELSON

P. 58: *Loretta Lynn performs, 1973.*
P. 59: *Loretta Lynn holding her ACM Artist of the Decade Award with her mother, Clara, and sister, Crystal Gayle.*
RIGHT: *Entertainer of the Year Merle Haggard performs, 1971.*

1980s

1980s

Dick Clark was a country fan at heart. Though millions of viewers knew him as a rock-n-roll icon on *American Bandstand*, Clark's first job was spinning records for a country station in Syracuse, New York. His first TV gig was on the country music show *Cactus Dick and the Santa Fe Riders*. Clark's country roots truly ran deep.

In 1979, Clark saw an opportunity in the budding Academy of Country Music Awards. After hosting the show in 1969, '71, '72, and '73, he moved behind the camera in 1979 to serve as executive producer and bring his own powerful dick clark company on to produce the event, continuing to work with producers Gene Weed and Ron Weed and talent producer Bill Boyd to build on what they had nurtured in the 1970s.

"I think my father saw that country music is really America's music," said Clark's son, R. A. "Rac" Clark, who first worked on the show under his father as a production coordinator in 1980. "As a businessman, he saw that he could help create something that would have a lasting value, which has proven true. One of the crown jewels of dick clark productions is still the Academy of Country Music Awards."

The early 1980s were ripe for Dick Clark's mainstream touch. The decade opened with country's favorite sons—Merle Haggard, Willie Nelson, and George Jones—back at the ACM podium. Jones, who had experienced a career lull after a string of hits (both solo and with his then-wife, Tammy Wynette) and a well-publicized divorce and battle with alcohol and drugs, staged a comeback with what would become his signature hit. The Billy Sherrill–produced "He Stopped Loving Her Today" won Song and Single Record of the Year in 1980 and brought Jones the trophy for Top Male Vocalist. Haggard's 1981 masterpiece album *Big City* earned him Top Male Vocalist of the Year honors for 1981 and the cut "Are the Good Times Really Over (I Wish a Buck Was Still Silver)" took home Song of the Year honors for 1982. Following his Entertainer of the Year win for 1979, Nelson solidified his status as a country innovator with the now classic "Always on My Mind," which earned him Single Record and Album of the Year honors for 1982, followed by two more consecutive Single Record of the Year wins for 1984 and 1985 (collaborations with Julio Iglesias and the Highwaymen, respectively).

P. 62: *George Strait performs, 1983.*
ABOVE: *ACM Male Vocalist George Jones, 1981.*
OPPOSITE: *Entertainer of the Year Willie Nelson performs, 1989.*

ABOVE: *Dolly Parton with Gene Weed and Bill Boyd, 1981.* BELOW: *Entertainer of the Year Barbara Mandrell with Male Vocalist of the Year George Jones, 1981.* OPPOSITE: *Barbara Mandrell and Eddie Rabbit perform.*

pop feel and image, from the no-holds-barred female perspective that women like Loretta Lynn, Tammy Wynette, and Dolly Parton had pioneered. Mandrell landed her own variety show on NBC with her sisters Louise and Irlene, giving the network a hit show and bringing country music into the living rooms of mainstream America. Barbara was named ACM Entertainer of the Year for 1980, becoming only the third woman to do so, after Loretta and Dolly.

"My fondest memory is the way everyone in the crew, and the cast of performers always made me feel welcome, at home, comfortable, and important," said Mandrell. "Television is so powerful, and it was a tremendous boost to my career to be on the ACM Awards show."

But in the early '80s country music was also garnering more attention from outside the genre, thanks in major part to the multitalented Barbara Mandrell. Playing pedal steel and saxophone and singing since childhood, Mandrell racked up the number one singles "Sleeping Single in a Double Bed," "(If Loving You Is Wrong) I Don't Want to Be Right," "I Was Country When Country Wasn't Cool," and "Crackers" (with the sexy line "You can eat crackers in my bed anytime") in the late '70s and early '80s. She sang with a more modern '80s

"Barbara was, in my opinion, the first big sea change in country music," remembered Barry Adelman, a writer for dick clark productions who would eventually join the ACM Awards show as a writer and producer. "Suddenly there was this really attractive, talented woman who was doing songs that were crossing over, and she was suddenly sought after on *Johnny Carson* and was somebody everybody wanted to book and have on their show."

COUNTRY ON THE SILVER SCREEN

While the Mandrell variety show was on the air and *Hee-Haw,* starring Buck Owens and Roy Clark, had also fought its way back to ratings success through syndication, country music began to move beyond TV and onto the silver screen with feature films like *Coal Miner's Daughter, 9 to 5, Honeysuckle Rose,* and *Urban Cowboy,* which were all released in 1980 and brought country themes and great music to a much wider audience. *Coal Miner's Daughter* won Sissy Spacek the Best Actress Oscar, and the Academy of Country Music named it Country Music Movie of the Year—a category that had only been established in 1979. In 1981, the award was renamed the Tex Ritter Film Award in honor of the Western film star and early Academy supporter, a nod to the Academy's early Western roots. His sons—*Three's Company* star John Ritter and his brother, Tom Ritter— presented the first renamed ACM trophy to Clint Eastwood's 1981 film *Any Which Way You Can.*

The movies on the big screen weren't only telling country tales; they were producing iconic country songs as well. *Honeysuckle Rose* featured what would become Willie Nelson's theme song "On the Road Again," *9 to 5* turned out Dolly Parton's Oscar-nominated working-woman title anthem, and *Urban Cowboy* made a star out of Johnny Lee with "Looking for Love." Lee was named Top New

TOP LEFT: *Buck Owens backstage, 1989.*
TOP RIGHT: *Three's Company's John Ritter (right) and brother Tom (left) present the ACM Tex Ritter Film Award to* Any Which Way You Can *director Buddy Van Horn, 1982.*
ABOVE: *Willie Nelson performs, 1983.*
OPPOSITE TOP: *Hosts Conway Twitty, Dottie West, and Mickey Gilley, 1982.*
OPPOSITE BOTTOM: *The Charlie Daniels Band performs, 1980.*

Male Vocalist for 1980, and the *Urban Cowboy* sound track—which featured the music of Mickey Gilley, the Charlie Daniels Band, Anne Murray, Bonnie Raitt, and Kenny Rogers—won Album of the Year at the 16th Annual ACM Awards.

"The *Urban Cowboy* movie was important because the biggest, hippest young star in America [John Travolta] put on a cowboy hat and western boots and danced to country music, legitimizing and making it hip in the minds of young people across the country, attracting many to the music," said Charlie Daniels of the *Urban Cowboy* phenomenon.

Gilley, who had dominated the ACM Awards in 1976 with five wins including Single Record, Song, Album, Top Male Vocalist of the Year, and Entertainer of the Year, continued his streak in the '80s with his club, Gilley's, winning Nightclub of the Year five times, thanks in part to *Urban Cowboy*. The club in Pasadena, Texas, had a starring role in the film, providing the energized location where Bud (Travolta) and Sissy (Debra Winger) fall in love to the sounds of a two-step and the taste of Lone Star beer.

ABOVE: *George Jones and Ray Charles duet, 1984.*
OPPOSITE TOP: *Oak Ridge Boys, 1981.*
OPPOSITE BOTTOM: *The Bellamy Brothers (left) with Johnny Lee and Razzy Bailey, 1981.*

"The *Urban Cowboy* movie was important because the biggest, hippest young star in America put on a cowboy hat and western boots and danced to country music, legitimizing and making it hip in the minds of young people."
—CHARLIE DANIELS

THE NEW TRADITIONALISTS

It was perhaps the success of *Urban Cowboy* that started the pendulum swing back toward a more traditional country sound. Though the music from the film was as genuine as could be, the influx of faux cowboys wearing jeans and boots and scooting their way across the floors at pop-up country bars in big cities across America made fans long for something they felt was somehow different. And the 1980s provided that in spades. A plethora of promising new male artists emerged, each bringing their own unique sound and brand of traditional country.

First up among the "new traditionalists" was a band that cut its teeth at the Bowery in Myrtle Beach, South Carolina, honing their skills under the name Alabama. Hailing from Fort Payne, Alabama, cousins Randy Owen, Teddy Gentry, and Jeff Cook, along with drummer Mark Herndon, brought a rocking edge to their music while keeping a "fiddle in the band" and singing about relatable country themes in hits like "Dixieland Delight," "Feels So Right," and "Tennessee River." A throwback to the "beer joint" bands that Merle Haggard described from the 1960s, Alabama was a bar band that became a national sensation.

"They were young, they were vibrant, they were good-looking, they were authentic, and they played music that was so catchy," said Adelman. "They were selling so many records, and they were sex symbols. They created excitement, and they were great showmen. We were fortunate, I think, in those years that they were one of the groups that really made the Academy of Country Music show something that everybody looked forward to."

Alabama won eighteen ACM Awards during the 1980s, including six consecutive trophies for Top Vocal Group of the Year and Entertainer of the Year. The band was named Artist of the Decade in 1988.

"The very first awards we ever got were from the ACMs," recalls the band's bassist Teddy Gentry. "We were adopted by Nashville later on, but I think the West Coast took us in under their wing and said yes to us even before Nashville did. We were kind of renegades, and I think we were looked at as kind of country rockers at the time with T-shirts and blue jeans and long hair. The industry was ready for a band to break through, though."

ABOVE: *Charley Pride, Randy Owen, Jeff Cook, and Carl Perkins join a backstage ACM jam, 1987.*
OPPOSITE: *Alabama's Randy Owen and Dukes of Hazzard star John Schneider.*

ARTIST OF THE DECADE
ALABAMA

The thing that our manager, Dale Morris, and I realized a long time ago is that network TV works the same out on the West Coast as it does in Nashville. In the 1980s, Dick Clark was at the helm of the Academy of Country Music Awards when it was coming to you from Knott's Berry Farm in Buena Park, and later, Universal Amphitheatre in Hollywood. Remember, Dick had done this a few times, so he knew what he was doing. And he was a great, great friend. Thanks to Dick, Alabama went from being a Southern rock honky-tonk group to being hip on *American Bandstand* and at the ACM Awards.

It felt great to have a relationship with Dick, as well as ACM executive director Bill Boyd and ACM Awards producer Gene Weed. I loved going out to LA and playing. That guitar doesn't know what city or state it's in. The ACMs were more laid-back. It was just different for me, and I think it was different for a lot of artists. The Academy of Country Music made you feel like you were appreciated because you made the effort to come out there and play and be a part of that. They used to say, "Well, there are no country music fans in Hollywood." Oh, hell yeah there are! The ACM Awards provided an opportunity to have these great stars—actors and other celebrities—come out and participate. Very, very smart and very great for country music.

We won our first ACM Award for 1980's Top Vocal Group. It was the first industry award we had ever won, and I thought that would be the last one. Seriously, it was much more than I ever expected. After that first win for 1980, Alabama went on to win seventeen other ACM Awards throughout the '80s. I even cohosted the show in 1993 with Reba McEntire and George Strait. In 1988, the Academy named us Artist of the Decade. That was amazing. It's a word a lot of people use, but we certainly never expected anything like that. Then, they surprised us again with the ACM Cliffie Stone Pioneer Award for pioneering strides in country music in 2002. Again, simply amazing to be in that great club with artists like Hank Williams, Johnny Cash, and Willie Nelson.

Over the years, Jeff, Teddy, and I certainly felt like we were a part of that process that built the ACM Awards into a hit program, and we took it very seriously. In country music we're blessed to have more than one national show dedicated to our stars. It's absolutely necessary because the competition makes it great for the artists. It helps us all rise. When we had our first number one song, "Tennessee River," it was like, "Well, this is really special but we don't expect another record at all." I just knew I wanted to work really hard and had my one opportunity and shot in life to not have to pick cotton and do things that I had grown up doing. Despite all our ACM wins, I never let myself celebrate in the early years because I was always so focused on what we were doing. We had so many shows and I had to be good for that next show, and I had to take care of my family and take care of my career. Now, looking back, I can enjoy all the accolades. I care a lot about the music. I still love the music, and I love performing. Good things happen when you stay humble and appreciative. I still feel that way in my heart. And I appreciate the Academy of Country Music.

–RANDY OWEN

ABOVE: *Alabama celebrates backstage, 1982.*
OPPOSITE TOP: *Alabama with the Artist of the Decade Award, 1989.*
OPPOSITE BOTTOM: *Alabama performs, 1983.*

RIGHT: *Dwight Yoakam and date, 1989.*
BELOW: *ACM Top New Male Vocalist nominees T. Graham Brown, Keith Whitley, Randy Travis, Marty Stuart and Billy Burnette, 1986.*
MIDDLE TOP: *Vince Gill with Sylvia (left) and Marie Osmond (right), 1985.*
MIDDLE BOTTOM: *Ronnie Milsap, 1984.*
FAR RIGHT: *ACM winner Ricky Skaggs behind the lens, 1985.*

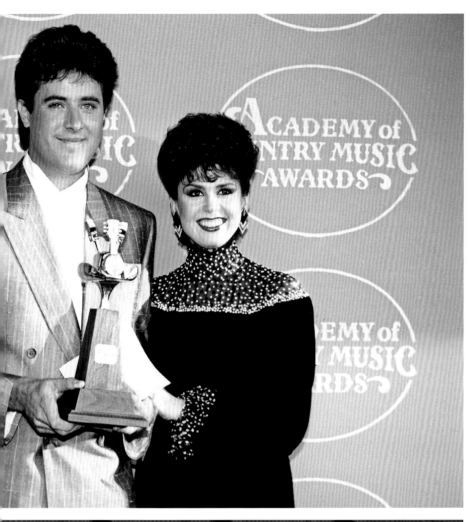

While embracing superstar acts like Alabama, the Academy also continued its longstanding tradition of spotlighting new talent, giving up-and-coming artists a shot at an abbreviated performance on the show. The '80s saw the debut of Ricky Skaggs, Keith Whitley, Marty Stuart, Ronnie Mislap, Larry Gatlin & the Gatlin Brothers and John Anderson, who would all go on to great success. Newcomers Vince Gill and Dwight Yoakam, who won their first industry awards as ACM Top New Male Vocalist for 1984 and 1986, respectively, would also reconnect the Academy to its West Coast roots. Gill, who was nineteen when he moved to Los Angeles to take a gig with Byron Berline's band Sundance, honed his musical skills in the thriving Southern California country rock scene of the late '70s and eventually joined the band Pure Prairie League.

"When I got there I was so glad that I went there," Gill reflected of his years in California. "It opened my mind up to the amazing world of music. That place was on fire. It was just kind of a really cool melting pot of all kinds of music. The country rock scene out there was massive. Boy, I soaked it all up and the people that I admired were out there. The lines were so blurred. Everybody was open-minded and willing."

Yoakam—whose unique style harkened back to '60s California country with a modern edge—had also found a welcoming home as an aspiring artist in Southern California, playing rock clubs as well as country bars. With songs like "Guitars, Cadillacs" and "Little Ways," Yoakam updated the honky-tonk tradition of Buck and Merle and breathed life into the Bakersfield Sound for a new generation. In 1988, Yoakam joined his hero Buck Owens for a performance of "Streets of Bakersfield" on the ACM Awards, a song they had already performed on the CMA Awards in Nashville.

"Oftentimes television shows won't do anything that somebody else has done first, but Bill Boyd and everyone at the ACMs said, 'We don't care. We own this. This is us. This is our birthright,'" recalled Yoakam. "It was really a glorious moment for me, to watch Buck kind of hold court on the stage of the organization that he helped to found. He really felt, I think, recrowned that night in that moment and acknowledged on national TV by the Academy of Country Music that his music was not forgotten."

Joining Gill and Yoakam among the future superstars who debuted in the '80s was George

Strait, who began his long run at the ACM Awards as Top Male Vocalist for 1984, winning six awards by decade's end, including the coveted Entertainer of the Year. A young upstart named Randy Travis also exploded, going from Top New Male Vocalist for 1985 to winning four trophies, including Top Male Vocalist and Single Record, Song and Album of the Year for 1986, on the strength of his monster hit "On the Other Hand."

OPPOSITE: *Dwight Yoakam, 1987.*
TOP: *Dwight Yoakam and Buck Owens sing "Streets of Bakersfield," 1988.*
ABOVE: *ACM Awards hosts George Strait, K.T. Oslin, and Patrick Duffy, 1989.*

ABOVE: *ACM Male Vocalist Randy Travis, 1987.*
OPPOSITE: *Merle Haggard sings "Twinkle, Twinkle Lucky Star," 1987.*

HOSTS & LOCATIONS

1980 • Loretta Lynn, Charley Pride & Claude Akins
KNOTT'S BERRY FARM, BUENA PARK, CA

1981 • Larry Gatlin, Tammy Wynette & Don Meredith
SHRINE AUDITORIUM, HOLLYWOOD, CA

1982 • Conway Twitty, Dottie West & Mickey Gilley
KNOTT'S BERRY FARM, BUENA PARK, CA

1983 • Jerry Reed, John Schneider & Tammy Wynette
KNOTT'S BERRY FARM, BUENA PARK, CA

1984 • Mac Davis, Crystal Gayle & Charley Pride
KNOTT'S BERRY FARM, BUENA PARK, CA

1985 • Glen Campbell, Janie Frickie & Loretta Lynn
KNOTT'S BERRY FARM, BUENA PARK, CA

1986 • Mac Davis, Reba McEntire & John Schneider
KNOTT'S BERRY FARM, BUENA PARK, CA

1987 • Patrick Duffy & The Judds
KNOTT'S BERRY FARM, BUENA PARK, CA

1988 • Reba McEntire & Hank Williams Jr.
KNOTT'S BERRY FARM, BUENA PARK, CA

1989 • Patrick Duffy, K. T. Oslin & George Strait
DISNEYLAND, ANAHEIM, CA

OPPOSITE: *Mac Davis, Reba McEntire, and John Schneider hosting, 1986.*

'80s LADIES

Another formidable family act in the '80s mix was a mother-daughter duo from the hills of Kentucky. After making a splash with "Mama He's Crazy" on their debut album in 1983, Naomi and Wynonna Judd arrived with a vengeance in 1984 with the album *Why Not Me*. The title cut from the album won the duo their first ACM Awards for Song of the Year and Top Vocal Duet, propelling them on a streak of seven straight wins for Vocal Duet. Naomi's glitz and sassy stage presence coupled with Wynonna's rebel spirit and full bluesy growl were the perfect combination for 1980s country fans.

TOP: *The Judds backstage, 1988.*
BELOW: *The Judds, 1985.*
OPPOSITE: *Sparkly Janie Fricke, Sylvia, Donna Fargo, Tammy Wynette, Reba McEntire, and Debby Boone, 1985.*

> "I think what country music was doing with this infusion of female voices was reflecting what was going on in the world around us."
> —HISTORIAN ROBERT K. OERMANN

The Judds weren't the only women making a splash at the ACM Awards during the decade. A young Oklahoma redhead named Reba McEntire debuted on the show in 1981 as a nominee for Top New Female Vocalist, losing the award to a red-hot Terri Gibbs and her monster hit "Somebody's Knockin'." But just a few short years later, Reba walked away with her first Top Female Vocalist trophy for 1984—the first of seven awards in that category, a record that still holds today. Reba was joined on the charts and the ACM Awards stage by other strong female performers, including K. T. Oslin, Kathy Mattea, Suzy Bogguss, and the trio of Dolly Parton,

OPPOSITE: *Reba dons a costume for "Cathy's Clown," 1989.*
LEFT: *Terri Gibbs, 1981.*
BOTTOM LEFT: *Hank Williams Jr., Reba, and Dick Clark, 1988.*
BOTTOM RIGHT: *Tammy Wynette, Reba, and Janie Fricke, backstage 1986.*

ABOVE LEFT: *Tanya Tucker performs, 1988.*
ABOVE RIGHT: *K.T. Oslin performs, 1989.*
BOTTOM RIGHT: *Mr. T. plays nanny for Crystal Gayle, 1984.*
OPPOSITE: *Dottie West duets with daughter, Shelly, 1983.*

Linda Ronstadt, and Emmylou Harris, who were winning not only female-designated categories but also general ones like Single Record and Song and Album of the Year.

"Without question the '80s was an era when female percentage of popularity on the charts in country music definitely increased and indeed reached the highest percentage it has ever been before or since," said Robert K. Oermann, country music historian and coauthor of *Finding Her Voice: Women in Country Music*. "I think women in the 1980s made tremendous strides in all areas of life, and what makes country music so interesting to me is that it so vividly reflects the culture. I think what country music was doing with this infusion of female voices was reflecting what was going on in the world around us."

I WANT MY CMT

The decade also ushered in a more youth-oriented aspect to country music, featuring artists who appealed to a younger fan who may have once considered country their parents' music. As the early '80s saw country music on the big screen, the mid-'80s saw it coming back to TV in the new short-form art known as music videos. MTV had caused an explosion with music

"I'm as gentle as a lamb and just as sweet as sugar, so you don't have to be afraid of me!"
—HANK WILLIAMS JR.

videos in pop and rock, and country fans got not one but two networks of their own in 1983. Hitting the airwaves within two days of each other were Country Music Television (CMT) and The Nashville Network (TNN), giving viewers both country videos and country lifestyle programming. To recognize this growing and important part of country music, the Academy added a Video of the Year category for 1984. The artist to take the first trophy was Hank Williams Jr., for the raucous clip "All My Rowdy Friends are Comin' Over Tonight." Surprisingly, the win was a first for "Bocephus," who had grown up as country royalty under the banner of his father Hank Williams', immense fame. That first win opened the floodgates for Williams, who was named Entertainer of the Year three straight years beginning with 1986. On his first Entertainer win, a clearly gleeful Hank accepted the trophy by acknowledging that, in his opinion, it had been a long time coming.

TOP: *Hank Williams Jr. performs on the ACM stage, 1985.*
BOTTOM LEFT: *Hank Jr. "duets" with the late Hank Sr., 1989.*
BOTTOM RIGHT: *Williams accepts his first Entertainer of the Year trophy, 1987.*

TOP LEFT: *Larry Gatlin and the Gatlin Brothers perform, 1980.*
TOP RIGHT: *Dwight Yoakam shares a laugh with Ashley, Naomi, and Wynonna Judd, 1987.*
BOTTOM LEFT: *Fleetwood Mac's Mick Fleetwood presents with Debra Allen, 1984.*
BOTTOM MIDDLE: *Dick Clark and Loretta Lynn review the script, 1989.*
BOTTOM RIGHT: *Randy Travis signs autographs for fans after his 1987 wins as then-wife and manager Lib Hatcher holds onto the trophies.*

"I have been around a while. I get the feeling that people were scared of me or the Academy was scared of me," Hank said onstage, eliciting laughter from the crowd. "I'm as gentle as a lamb and just as sweet as sugar, so you don't have to be afraid of me!"

As the decade wrapped, another group of young artists arrived on the country scene—a group that would change the face of country and be forever known as "The Class of '89." The core of this group—Clint Black, Alan Jackson, Travis Tritt, and Garth Brooks—was making music that would take country to places it never imagined in the 1990s.

ACM Entertainer *of the* Year Winners

1980
BARBARA MANDRELL

1981
ALABAMA

1982
ALABAMA

1983
ALABAMA

1984
ALABAMA

1985
ALABAMA

1986
HANK WILLIAMS JR.

1987
HANK WILLIAMS JR.

1988
HANK WILLIAMS JR.

1989
GEORGE STRAIT

LEFT: *Entertainer of the Year George Strait, 1986.*

1990s

1990s

Just a few minutes into the 1990 Academy of Country Music Awards broadcast, it was clear the "Class of '89" had arrived. Although it was their first time to appear on the show, newcomers Clint Black and Garth Brooks (who had both debuted on the country scene in 1989) were nominated in just about every category. Brooks had recently hit the Top 10 with his debut

single "Much Too Young (To Feel This Damn Old)." Black, riding high on his number one debut single "A Better Man," would take home trophies for Top New Male Vocalist as well as Top Male Vocalist, Album of the Year, and Single Record of the Year.

"We all felt like that awards show was a huge catalyst," Black reflected. "You know songs on the radio are doing something and you know that records are being sold, but we also knew that nothing had an impact like television did, and the ACMs were, for me, the biggest shot on television I had ever had. I had a concert in Texas the night after and brought the award out on stage—which for most of us country music fans, you don't even get close to an award. So, it was exciting for me to walk out on stage and hold that award out there and show it to the audience."

After watching Black repeatedly walk to the podium that night, Brooks got a pep talk from the Academy's Bill Boyd and longtime ACM Awards producer Gene Weed.

"I remember Bill and Gene were very sweet to me that first year when Clint Black cleaned up," Brooks would later reflect. "I'm sitting there with my head down, Gene came up and put his arm around me and said, 'Don't worry, your time is coming.'"

Boy, was it ever. In 1991, Garth returned to the ACM Awards in a swoop of glory. In only one year, the Oklahoma native had earned himself four number one singles, so many that he had to sing a medley of his hits to satisfy the fans watching at home. Garth wrapped all his influences—from Merle Haggard and George Jones to James Taylor and Billy Joel—into his music, and he brought an arena rock sensibility to his live performances. It wasn't unusual to see him jumping off the stage or flying over fans in the packed stadiums he would play. Fans were camping out to buy tickets to his shows, landing Garth on the cover of *Rolling Stone*—still a rarity at that time for a country act.

P. 96: *Garth Brooks performs*
ABOVE: *Buck Owens and Clint Black see eye to eye, 1991.*
OPPOSITE: *Clint Black, 1991.*

"A lot of us were brought up on Merle and Buck, but also on the Eagles and Bob Seger and Skynyrd and great rock-n-roll . . . We were bringing different sensibilities to that traditional country music."
—CLINT BLACK

Garth won every ACM Award he was nominated for in 1991, including Entertainer of the Year. It was an early glimpse at the Garth domination to come. His second album, *No Fences*, would go on to sell more than thirteen million copies, and his third album, *Ropin' the Wind*, was the first country album to debut at the top of the pop albums chart. Not since Willie Nelson, Waylon Jennings, Jessi Colter, and Tompall Glaser broke the million-selling mark with *Wanted! The Outlaws* in 1976 had country music moved so many records. In 1992, even *Forbes* covered Garth's meteoric rise, featuring the headline "Country Conquers Rock."

RIGHT: *Garth Brooks, 1991.*
BELOW: *Garth Brooks performs with sister Betsy Smittle and friend Ty England, 1993.*
OPPOSITE TOP: *George Strait and Dick Clark at rehearsals, 1991.*
OPPOSITE BOTTOM: *Clint Black, 1994.*

Garth's seemingly overnight triumph was the perfect theme for country music in the 1990s. The entire decade seemed to be in overdrive, taking brand-new artists and making them superstars in a matter of months instead of years. Brooks, Black, Alan Jackson, and the other members of the now legendary "Class of '89"were unique singer-songwriters who each brought his own sound and style to a growing genre.

"A lot of us were brought up on Merle and Buck, but also on the Eagles and Bob Seger and Skynyrd and great rock 'n' roll. So we were bringing different sensibilities to that traditional country music," Black explains. "It was like the perfect storm. I remember when SoundScan started registering sales and everyone had to look and say 'Oh, country music sells.'"

AROUND THE WORLD
AND BACK AGAIN

Country music had seemingly found the perfect mix of real and commercial, and fans couldn't get enough. Record labels were releasing new artists as quickly as possible, and platinum album parties were a common sight on Nashville's Music Row, with everyone reaping the benefits of country's new mainstream popularity. While younger fans began migrating over to country music in the '80s, the '90s provided even more bait to a new generation of listeners. The face of country music was decidedly hipper, and for the first time young fans not only saw artists who looked more like them, they also heard music made by people who had grown up on the same varied rock and pop music they had. Suddenly teenagers who were listening to Bon Jovi and Duran Duran in the '80s found something to pique their interest in the pure voice of Vince Gill, the earnestness of Brooks, or the rockin' edge of Tritt and Marty Stuart. Country had found its way into pop culture, truly becoming "America's

OPPOSITE TOP: *Top Vocal Group Little Texas, 1994.*
OPPOSITE MIDDLE: *Tracy Byrd, Chely Wright, and Clay Walker present, 1996.*
OPPOSITE BOTTOM: *Vince Gill faces the press, 1995.*
TOP: *Travis Tritt and Marty Stuart, 1996.*
BOTTOM LEFT: *Travis Tritt performs "Bible Belt" with actor Joe Pesci, 1992.*
BOTTOM RIGHT: *Top Vocal Group Diamond Rio, 1993.*

STAFF PASS

ALL ACCESS

Does Not Entitle
Bearer to theatre
Seat

PRESS PASS

Press Area Only!
No Holding Area
No Green Room
No Stage
No Dressing Rooms
Does Not Entitle Bearer
to theatre Seat

CREW PASS

ALL ACCESS

Does Not Entitle
Bearer to theatre
Seat

GUEST PASS

Green Room Tent - ok
No Stage
No Dressing Rooms
No Holding Area
Does Not Entitle Bearer
to theatre Seat

TALENT PASS

ALL Access

Does Not Entitle
Bearer to theatre
Seat

TALENT ESCORT PASS

ALL access

Does Not Entitle Bearer
to theatre Seat

LEFT: *Alabama, 1998.*
TOP: *Doug Supernaw, Tracy Lawrence, Aaron Tippin and Toby Keith have fun at the All-Star Jam, 1995.*
ABOVE: *The backstage passes grid, 1991.*

LEFT: *Mark Chesnutt, Tim McGraw, and Tracy Lawrence at the All-Star Jam, 1993.*
BOTTOM: *Toby Keith, 1999.*
OPPOSITE TOP: *Kenny Chesney accepts his first ACM Award in 1998 with mom Karen (right) and presenters Kathy Mattea and Charley Pride.*
OPPOSITE BOTTOM: *ACM Award winners Charlie Daniels, Bryan White, Toby Keith, and Montgomery Gentry, 1999.*

music" after so long being considered a regional art form. Country radio grew to become the largest radio format in the nation, sharing the music of this new generation of artists from coast to coast. Although the breakout country music artists of the '90s continued to echo the sounds of influences like Haggard and Jones, the music overall went from "three chords and the truth" to "three chords and a party."

"This is the time when the larger music business really stood up and paid attention," said country music historian Robert K. Oermann. "Cover stories in *Forbes* and *Time* magazines said this format was booming, and it was. Profits tripled between 1989 and 1995. The amount of money that was being generated by country music was just astounding. It was completely unprecedented, and it made the larger culture sit up and pay attention."

Riding the wave of country's 1990s tsunami, the Academy of Country Music Awards also gained a larger audience, swelling to twenty million viewers in 1997 and giving the platform even more clout to help break new acts. Among the artists to receive their first industry recognition at the ACM Awards were future stars Kenny Chesney, Tracy Lawrence, and Tim McGraw.

"I think fans love to see the ACM Awards, and to see their favorite artists. It's like the country music Oscars."
—TRISHA YEARWOOD

Continuing the strides on the ACMs made by artists like Loretta Lynn, Tammy Wynette, Barbara Mandrell, K. T. Oslin, and Kathy Mattea, a new generation of women also emerged in the '90s, building on that female power and taking it full tilt. Mary Chapin Carpenter, Patty Loveless, Faith Hill, Martina McBride, Pam Tillis, Trisha Yearwood, Lee Ann Womack, and Lorrie Morgan were among the newcomers who spoke to women everywhere. The Dixie Chicks also brought their own sass to the scene, giving country music an energy and cool look that young girls wanted to copy.

"I think it just feels like acceptance. It's a sign of success, that you've made it," said Yearwood, who won her first ACM Award for 1991's Top New Female Vocalist. "I think fans love to see the ACM Awards, and to see their favorite artist. It's like the country music Oscars . . . what's everybody wearing, who's gonna win. It's fun."

ABOVE: *Trisha Yearwood performs with The Mavericks' Raul Malo, 1997.*
LEFT: *Lorrie Morgan and Roger Miller, 1992.*
FAR LEFT: *ACM Award winner Patty Loveless, 1998.*
OPPOSITE TOP LEFT: *Trisha Yearwood, 1998.*
OPPOSITE TOP RIGHT: *Martina McBride, 1994.*
OPPOSITE BOTTOM: *Lee Ann Womack, 1999.*

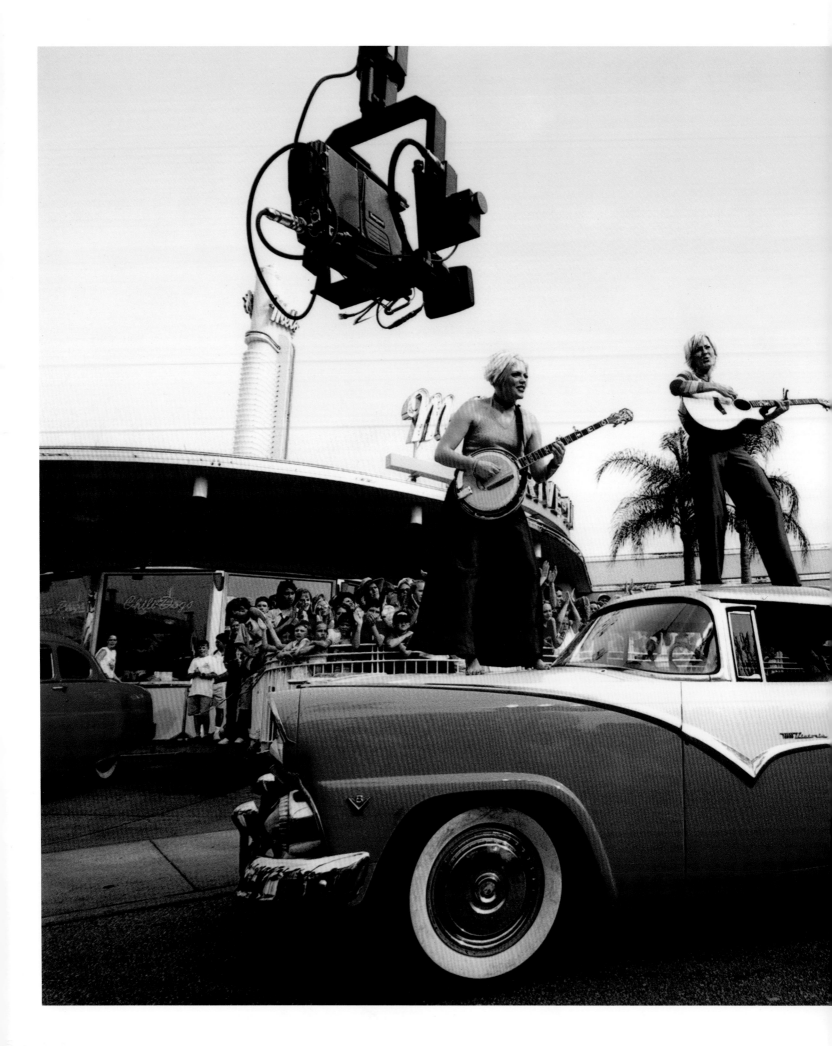

TOP: *Garth Brooks and Chris LeDoux perform, 1997.*
ABOVE: *Bryan White performs, 1997.*
LEFT: *The Dixie Chicks shoot their newcomer nominee video for the 1999 ACM Awards.*

TIM & FAITH

Tim McGraw and Faith Hill shared one of their most private and poignant moments on live TV with ACM Awards viewers. Hill was named New Female Vocalist of the Year for 1993 and McGraw won New Male Vocalist for 1994, so both their stars were on the rise when they married in October 1996. At the 1997 ACM Awards, the newlyweds debuted their song "It's Your Love," which had just been sent to radio the week prior, in a memorable live performance. It was set to be released on Tim's new album *Everywhere* that next June. As the two took to the stage, Faith was three weeks away from delivering their first child, and she and Tim sang the passionate song directly to each other.

"The first debut of a song that was really a big deal to me was Faith and me doing 'It's Your Love' together on the ACMs," said McGraw. "It was the first time that anybody had seen us perform that song and she was pregnant at the time—I mean *really* pregnant with Gracie. So that was the first time I remember having a debut song that really meant something big to me."

"It was one of the best moments of my life," Hill said of the performance. "Other than praying that I wouldn't go into early labor, it was truly a fairy-tale moment for me."

OPPOSITE: *Tim McGraw and Faith Hill perform "It's Your Love" in 1997.*
TOP: *Faith Hill wins Top New Female Vocalist, 1994.*
ABOVE: *Tim and Faith accept Single Record of the Year, 1998.*
BOTTOM: *Faith performs solo, 1999.*

SHANIA'S TRIUMPH

While Tim and Faith were capturing the fans' attention in a way that no husband-and-wife duo in country music had since Tammy Wynette and George Jones or Johnny Cash and June Carter Cash before them, it was Canadian Shania Twain who would join Garth in breaking many long-held conventions of the genre. Bursting onto the country charts with "Whose Bed Have Your Boots Been Under?" and "Any Man of Mine" in 1995, she bared her midriff and made music with her then rock producer husband Robert John "Mutt" Lange. Her tunes of female empowerment were perfect for girls' nights out, giving young, professional women an anthem for their modern lives. Her beauty, style, and fearlessness made country attractive to the mainstream press, exposing the genre to a wider audience, much as Garth Brooks had done before her. She made her first appearance at the ACM Awards sitting atop a piano and singing the catchy "No One Needs to Know" just before winning ACM Top New Female Vocalist. Her album, *The Woman in Me*, would go on to sell more than ten million copies and was named ACM Album of the Year for 1995.

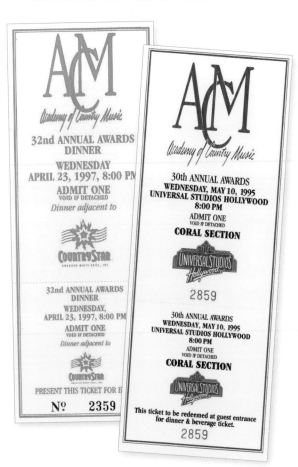

ABOVE: *Shania performs "No One Needs to Know" in 1996.*
LEFT: *Shania on the red carpet, 1999.*
OPPOSITE: *Shania accepts Top New Female Vocalist in 1996.*

29th ANNUAL
ACADEMY OF
COUNTRY MUSIC
★ Awards Dinner ★
UNIVERSAL STUDIOS • HOLLYWOOD
TUESDAY • MAY 3, 1994 • 8:00 PM

Shania and other new artists capitalized on the "MTV culture" that had become mainstream in the 1990s, using the visual format to help propel her as artist. What started as a novelty in the 1980s was now a necessity for any artist and helped break many newcomers into the mainstream. It was the music video for "Achy Breaky Heart" that helped make Billy Ray Cyrus a near-overnight superstar. After years of "hat acts," Cyrus was a different breed, with skintight jeans, tennis shoes, and a mullet haircut that would become legendary.

OPPOSITE: *Billy Ray Cyrus on the ACM Awards, 1993.*
TOP: *Billy Ray Cyrus with producers Gene Weed and Bill Boyd, 1993.*
BOTTOM: *Billy Ray Cyrus with Bob and Nan Kingsley (right), 1993.*

HOSTS & LOCATIONS

1990 · Alabama, The Judds, George Strait & Tammy Wynette
UNIVERSAL AMPHITHEATRE, HOLLYWOOD, CA

1991 · Clint Black, Kathy Mattea & George Strait
UNIVERSAL AMPHITHEATRE, HOLLYWOOD, CA

1992 · Clint Black, Lorrie Morgan & Travis Tritt
UNIVERSAL AMPHITHEATRE, HOLLYWOOD, CA

1993 · Randy Owen, Reba McEntire & George Strait
UNIVERSAL AMPHITHEATRE, HOLLYWOOD, CA

1994 · Reba McEntire & Alan Jackson
UNIVERSAL AMPHITHEATRE, HOLLYWOOD, CA

1995 · Clint Black, Tanya Tucker & Jeff Foxworthy
UNIVERSAL AMPHITHEATRE, HOLLYWOOD, CA

1996 · Brooks & Dunn, Faith Hill & Crystal Bernard
UNIVERSAL AMPHITHEATRE, HOLLYWOOD, CA

1997 · George Strait, Crystal Bernard & Jeff Foxworthy
UNIVERSAL AMPHITHEATRE, HOLLYWOOD, CA

1998 & 1999 · No Hosts
UNIVERSAL AMPHITHEATRE, HOLLYWOOD, CA

OPPOSITE: *Clint Black and George Strait, 1991.*

KIX & RONNIE

The decade also saw the rise of a new dominant country music duo that would go on to make ACM history. After the Judds called it quits in 1991 because of Naomi's health struggles with hepatitis C, Brooks & Dunn were there to fill that void with a rockin' honky-tonk sound that appealed to both men and women. Their debut single, "Brand New Man" helped earn them the trophy for ACM Top New Vocal Duet or Group, as well as overall Top Vocal Duet—a category they would go on to win a record sixteen times.

"The ACMs were the first awards we ever won," said Kix Brooks. "I remember 'Neon Moon' went number one the week we won, and the next week our record sales went from ten thousand a week to twenty thousand and we never looked back! We celebrated real hard, and I carried my awards around with me all night. The next morning I woke up in my hotel room and those two awards were sitting there all beat up from getting carried around together. "

OPPOSITE: *Brooks & Dunn perform, 1993.*
TOP: *Brooks & Dunn clean up, 1992.*
LEFT: *Kix Brooks and Ronnie Dunn with legendary songwriter and ACM supporter Mae Boren Axton, 1994.*

TOP: *Buddies Steve Wariner and Garth Brooks perform, 1999.* OPPOSITE: *Reba McEntire and Vince Gill, 1993.*

"It was one of the best nights of my life," remembers Ronnie Dunn. "I don't remember what I said when we got to the microphone. I remember turning around to walk backstage fighting back tears. Kix and I couldn't look at one another for a few minutes. We had both fought long and hard to pay our dues. That award marked the beginning of a long, successful ride."

"I remember 'Neon Moon' went number one the week we won, and the next week our record sales went from ten thousand a week to twenty thousand a week and we never looked back!"
—KIX BROOKS

Along with the many new acts making names for themselves, superstars Reba McEntire, Vince Gill, and George Strait continued cranking out hits in the '90s, keeping the foundation strong for traditional country. Reba, who brought to the show a Broadway sensibility with dramatic performances, dancers, and costume changes, was named

Top Female Vocalist of the Year three times during that decade and would win Entertainer of the Year in 1994. Vince's dry humor, combined with heart-wrenching country songs, earned him two wins for Top Male Vocalist as well as Song of the Year for "I Still Believe in You." Following up his own Entertainer win in 1989, George would go on to win both Top Male Vocalist and Album of the Year honors twice each during the decade, further establishing himself as a country king.

Though the '90s established legendary country artists and talented newcomers alike, the decade truly belonged to Brooks. His magic combination of great songs, energetic stage presence, and humble demeanor made him not only a star in the States, but around the world. His international tours in Europe and massive concert in New York's Central Park were historic in nature, proving that good country music truly had no boundaries. The Academy of Country Music rewarded his incredible worldwide success with the Artist of the Decade trophy in 1998.

ARTIST OF THE DECADE
GARTH BROOKS

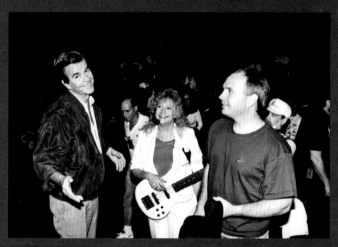

OPPOSITE: *Garth Brooks performs.*
TOP: *Dick Clark with Garth Brooks at rehearsal, 1992.*
ABOVE: *Garth Brooks with ACM Artist of the Decade Award.*

It would be hard to deny the statement that the '90s was the biggest decade in country music's history, and it was exciting to be a part of it. The ACM Awards were a highlight of every year. We went away empty-handed the first year we were ever nominated for anything, but I felt like the big winner thanks to the new relationships I had formed with Gene Weed and Bill Boyd—two guys who treated me like their son—a cherished page in the book of my life. It would be the next year, 1991, that we would walk away with awards for Single Record (Friends in Low Places), Song ("The Dance"), Album (No Fences), Video ("The Dance"), Top Male Vocalist, and Entertainer of the Year, truly a big, big night for my career, and what I believe was the launching pad for our run in the '90s.

In 1992, the ACM Awards show would be part of world history, as during the airing of the show, the Los Angeles riots would begin. I remember Travis Tritt coming into the dressing room telling us to turn on the news. We all watched as the results of the Rodney King verdict swept through the city. As the bus was pulling out of the awards show that evening, the beginnings of a song would start to form, inspired by the LA riots. We stopped at the Grand Canyon the next day. I stepped into a phone booth to call songwriter Stephanie Davis. When she answered and I asked, "Are you watching what is going on in Los Angeles?" she said, "I am way ahead of you. The song is called, 'We Shall Be Free'."

As the decade continued, my relationship with Dick Clark grew from strictly business to a true, true friendship . . . what a sweet soul. With the passing of Bill Boyd, my relationship with Fran Boyd also grew, as her role in the ACM Awards became more full-time. The new guard, Rac Clark and Bob Romeo, would truly feel like brothers, and that feeling continues to grow stronger today. When anyone asks me what is the difference between awards shows, I always try to explain that some represent the beliefs more of the industry and some represent the beliefs more of the people, and I think we need them both. The ACM Awards have always seemed to be the voice of the people reacting to the nominations that come from the industry, a good balance, in my opinion.

My greatest memories of the ACM Awards have to be those that I've made with the fellow entertainers I've been fortunate enough to be around: Jones, Haggard, Loretta, Strait, Reba, and LeDoux to name a few. I thought receiving the Artist of the Decade award from the Academy, presented to me by the great Alabama, was my favorite memory, but it would be rivaled by presenting that same award to King George a decade later.

The greatest of the greatest line the historic halls of the Academy of Country Music. To have your name in there somewhere is quite a compliment and an honor.

–GARTH BROOKS

THE END OF AN ERA

While the face and sound of country music were changing, the Academy of Country Music Awards was undergoing some changes behind the scenes. In February 1995, longtime ACM executive director Bill Boyd died at his home after a massive heart attack. His wife, Academy of Country Music staffer Fran Boyd, stepped into his role as executive director and as talent coordinator for the show. After being broadcast on NBC since the 1970s, the ACM Awards moved to CBS in 1998. And in August 1999, longtime ACM Awards producer and director Gene Weed lost his battle with cancer. Dick Clark's son, R. A. "Rac" Clark, moved back to Los Angeles to join the ACM Awards after spending five years in Nashville producing the nightly TNN variety show *Prime Time Country*. It was the end of an era and the beginning of a new one for the Academy of Country Music Awards as the millennium arrived, setting the scene for a major move to come.

OPPOSITE TOP LEFT: *John Anderson and Tracy Lawrence.*
OPPOSITE RIGHT: *George Jones and Buck Owens arrive, 1993.*
OPPOSITE MIDDLE: *Garth Brooks, Doug Stone, ACM's Fran Boyd and Neal McCoy at rehearsals, 1999.*
OPPOSITE BOTTOM: *ACM Pioneer Award winner Johnny Cash is celebrated by wife June Carter Cash, Marie Osmond, and Academy Award-winning actor Robert DuVall, 1991.*
ABOVE: *ACM Executive Director Bill Boyd.*
LEFT: *Fran Boyd, 1993.*

ACM Entertainer
of the **Year Winners**

1990
GARTH BROOKS

1991
GARTH BROOKS

1992
GARTH BROOKS

1993
GARTH BROOKS

1994
REBA McENTIRE

1995
BROOKS & DUNN

1996
BROOKS & DUNN

1997
GARTH BROOKS

1998
GARTH BROOKS

1999
SHANIA TWAIN

LEFT: *Entertainer of the Year Reba McEntire.*

2000s

2000s

As the year 2000 rolled in, people around the world waited anxiously for the Y2K chaos that never came. The new millennium got off to a smooth start, but the decade would bring some monumental changes for both America and for the Academy of Country Music. After the passing of longtime ACM Awards producer and director Gene Weed, producers Rac Clark and Barry

Adelman stepped up to helm the show under executive producers Dick Clark and Al Schwartz. Rac had grown up working on his father's shows, starting as production coordinator for the ACM Awards in 1980.

"My earliest memory of the ACM Awards is skateboarding through the Shrine Auditorium," Rac said. "I was a production coordinator when we moved from Knott's Berry Farm to the Shrine, and the production office was so far away from the bathrooms that I took the skateboard across that rink of the exhibition hall."

The strong relationships Clark forged while working on *Prime Time Country* in Nashville would serve him well as a producer on the ACM Awards.

Adelman, a Chicago native, had been a longtime writer for dick clark productions and had added producing duties for premiere properties such as the *Golden Globes* and *Dick Clark's New Year's Rockin' Eve* to his plate. Barry was a

mentor to Rac along with Gene and Dick, and he watched Rac work his way through the ranks.

Rac and Barry were a formidable duo from the start, and they came together just as country music was experiencing a big loss and another big wave of crossover success. After burning up the charts for a decade, touring around the world, and becoming one of the top-selling artists of all time, Garth Brooks announced in 2000 that he was retiring from recording and touring to spend time raising his girls on his Oklahoma ranch. The same year, Faith Hill and Lonestar had each charted career songs that were hits on both the country and Top 40 charts. The provocative single "Breathe" was named the *Billboard*'s number one single of 2000, helping earn Hill ACM Top Female Vocalist and Video of the Year trophies. Lonestar's power ballad "Amazed" also made *Billboard*'s year-end Top 10 for 2000 and won both ACM Song and Single Record of the Year.

P. 130: *Taylor Swift performs at the ACM All Star Jam, 2009.*
ABOVE: *Dick Clark with son and fellow producer Rac Clark, 2001.*
OPPOSITE: *Faith Hill, 2005.*

"I always felt uncomfortable about the attention this song has brought to me. I guess I was always uncomfortable about what it was written about."

—ALAN JACKSON, on "Where Were You (When the World Stopped Turning)"

Dixie Chicks' *Fly* was garnering attention from a wide range of fans due to the band's musical prowess and spunky attitude, earning ACM Album of the Year honors in 2000. And Lee Ann Womack was enjoying both a pop and country hit with her thought-provoking ballad "I Hope You Dance" (featuring band Sons of the Desert), which took home Single Record, Song, and Vocal Event of the Year for 2000. The show that year was hosted, appropriately enough, by ten-time ACM Award winner Dolly Parton—one of country's original crossover acts.

9/11

While country music was strong in the early 2000s, its mettle would be tested along with the rest of the nation on September 11, 2001, when Al-Qaeda terrorists on the orders of Osama bin Laden hijacked four planes and crashed them into the World Trade Center in New York City, the Pentagon in Washington, D.C., and a Pennsylvania field, killing more than three thousand innocent men, women, and children. A shocked nation looked for comfort, and some of country's finest artists, also moved by the unbelievably tragic events of that day, poured their anger and grief into music. Alan Jackson's "Where Were You (When the World Stopped Turning)" expressed the fear and confusion felt by many Americans, asking how something so evil could happen to thousands of innocent people. His message of hope in the face of unspeakable horror gave solace at a time when the nation needed it most. The song would garner Single Record and Song of the Year honors for Alan at the 2002 ACM Awards.

"I've always felt uncomfortable about the attention this song has brought to me. I guess I was always uncomfortable about what it was written about," said the usually soft-spoken Jackson as he accepted Song of the Year. "I'm still angry and sad and forever changed about what happened that day, and I thank God for sending the words and music down to me because I believe I was an instrument for that for some reason. I don't feel like I can accept the award for this song without sharing it with and dedicating it to the thousands of people, men and women and children, that died and suffered and are still suffering because of that cowardly and heartless attack on America and mankind. So this is for all of them."

Three-time ACM Award Winner Toby Keith was also angry, and he expressed that anger in a different way. In early 2002, Keith released "Courtesy of the Red, White, & Blue (The Angry American)," which in no uncertain terms called for retaliation against those responsible for the 9/11

OPPOSITE TOP LEFT: *Lonestar, 2000.*
OPPOSITE BOTTOM LEFT: *Lee Ann Womack celebrates "I Hope You Dance" with Sons of the Desert's Drew Womack, 2001.*
OPPOSITE RIGHT: *ACM Awards host Dolly Parton.*
ABOVE: *Alan Jackson performs, 2001.*

attacks. Keith's song reflected the call for justice that swept the nation, but it became the center of an unintended controversy. In an August 2002 interview with the *Los Angeles Daily News*, Dixie Chicks' singer Natalie Maines was quoted criticizing Keith's song, saying, "It's ignorant, and it makes country music sound ignorant."

During a 2002 interview with CMT.com, Keith was asked about Maines' remarks. "I'm a songwriter. She's not," he said. "She can say my song is ignorant, then it's ignorant for her to say that because she's not a songwriter."

The debate would show up on the live Academy of Country Music Awards in 2003. Performing with the Dixie Chicks via satellite from Austin, Texas, Maines wore a T-shirt with the letters F.U.T.K. on the front. The band would at first publicly say the letters stood for "Freedom, Understanding, Tolerance, and Knowledge," but many viewers thought it was a slam at Keith, including presenter Vince Gill. As he announced the winner for ACM Entertainer of the Year, Gill quipped, "Well, I think his name was on someone's shirt tonight, Toby Keith."

OPPOSITE: *Alan Jackson, 2001.*
ABOVE: *Toby Keith, 2002.*
BELOW: *Toby Keith performs "Courtesy of the Red, White & Blue (The Angry American)," 2002.*

VEGAS GOES COUNTRY

That same year, the Academy would undergo one of the biggest changes in its history. After thirty-seven years in Los Angeles, the ACM Awards moved to a new city for the first time—Las Vegas. The momentous move in 2003 was precipitated by a shortage of whisky at an LA hotel bar the year prior.

"Our board president Jack Lameier and I were having a drink before the show, and they ran out of Crown Royal," recalled Bob Romeo, who was the Academy's board chairman at the time. "We couldn't believe it. Who would run out of Crown? Jack said, 'I bet I know one place that wouldn't run out of Crown—Vegas!'"

What started as a joke over pre-show cocktails quickly turned into a serious proposition. On May 21, 2003, the Academy moved its television property to the Mandalay Bay Events Center on the world-famous Las Vegas Strip—broadcasting its new location live on CBS. What had been dubbed "Country Music's Party of the Year" *really* became a party, sprinkling the country show with a little Vegas glitz. The move propelled the ACM Awards to a bigger audience, both at home and live in the venue. Three shows later, after celebrating the show's fortieth anniversary, the Academy was forced to move once again to the larger MGM Grand Garden Arena to handle ticket demand.

"I remember we were scared to death that we couldn't even sell out Mandalay Bay," recalls Gayle Holcomb, an agent at WME and longtime ACM chairman, who championed the move to Vegas. "We were going from 6,000 seats at Universal Amphitheatre to 7,800 at Mandalay. But it took off like a rocket. It's amazing to think how quickly we went from Mandalay Bay to selling out 12,000 seats at MGM."

With the big move came some other big changes. The ACM "hat" trophy that had been used in some version since 1968 was redesigned by Grammy-winning art director Bill Johnson (who also designed the iconic *Rolling Stone* magazine logo). The new design was sleeker and more contemporary but retained the image of the cowboy hat in the trophy's top view as homage to the organization's past. Also in 2003, another era came to a close. After thirty-five years with the Academy—eight as executive director—Fran Boyd retired from the show she called "her baby." She says her legacy is the new artists she helped step into the spotlight.

"We wanted to put as many country artists on that show come hell or high water than any show you could turn the TV set on to watch," Boyd said of her years with the Academy. "And we did it. People would say 'Why is it that you baby these new artists?' I said, 'I don't baby them. New artists need to get out and get on the road and make a living. So I've just given them the extra time that they need to push themselves a little bit harder.'"

OPPOSITE TOP: *Brad Paisley and Alison Krauss perform "Whiskey Lullaby," 2004.* OPPOSITE BOTTOM: *Three-time ACM Female Vocalist of the Year Martina McBride performs, 2007.* TOP: *Gayle Holcomb, Bob Romeo, and Jack Lameier at Las Vegas' Mandalay Bay Events Center, 2003.* ABOVE: *2002 VIP pass.*

COUNTRY'S NEXT SUPERSTARS

Giving new artists a chance to shine has been a trademark of the ACM Awards from the beginning and continued on in the 2000s. Among the future superstars who stepped onto the ACM stage for the first time were Jason Aldean, Miranda Lambert, Luke Bryan, Keith Urban, Dierks Bentley, Brad Paisley, Rascal Flatts, Carrie Underwood, Blake Shelton, Taylor Swift, Big & Rich, Zac Brown Band, Lady Antebellum, Little Big Town, and Sugarland.

Kristian Bush of Sugarland remembers their first ACM performance in 2005 vividly. The group (then a trio with Bush, Jennifer Nettles, and Kristen Hall) had just released its debut single "Baby Girl" and were in Vegas to take advantage of radio interviews on site at the show. They got a call from the producers to come close the show after another performer got sick.

Pp. 140–141: *Buddy Owens, Blink 182's Travis Barker, Dwight Yoakam, Chris Hillman, Brad Paisley, Buckaroo Tom Brumley, and ZZ Top's Billy Gibbons pay tribute to the late Buck Owens at the 2006 ACM Awards.*
TOP: *Zac Brown Band at the All-Star Jam, 2009.*
ABOVE: *Little Big Town at the New Artists Show, 2006.*
OPPOSITE: *Carrie Underwood celebrates her first ACM Entertainer of the Year win at the All-Star Jam, 2009.*

"We were like, 'Nobody knows us! We're going to close the ACMs on national television? We're going to lose our minds,'" Bush recalls. "That was our first big performance on television in front of the country music community and the artists and the fans, and it was amazing. We didn't know we were going to be on television, so we were throwing on clothes that we had with us, and Jennifer tried to borrow some shoes, it was maybe Sara Evans' shoes or something, and they just didn't fit, so she kicked them off and went out barefoot. It was pretty funny! If you look at the rerun, we were terrified."

Bombastic duo Big & Rich were anything but terrified when they first rolled into the ACM Awards the year prior. John Rich—formerly of Lonestar—and "Big Kenny" Alphin discovered a musical kinship as singers and songwriters, joining as a duo and creating a thriving salon of like-minded musicians called the Muzik Mafia that played weekly at Nashville's Pub of Love. The

OPPOSITE: *Rascal Flatts, 2008.*
LEFT: *Sugarland makes their ACM Awards debut in 2005.*
BOTTOM: *Big and Rich with "hick hop" innovator Cowboy Troy performing "Save a Horse, Ride a Cowboy," 2004.*

ABOVE: *Taylor Swift meets Tim McGraw and Faith Hill on live TV, 2007.*
RIGHT: *Taylor Swift performs.*
OPPOSITE TOP: *Jennifer Nettles wins ACM Song of the Year as the composer of "Stay."*
OPPOSITE BOTTOM: *Newcomer Miranda Lambert rocks out at the All-Star Jam, 2006.*

pair debuted their second single "Save a Horse (Ride a Cowboy)" at the 39th ACM Awards, arriving to the red carpet on horseback. The song's in-your-face mix of country, hip hop and rap was a harbinger of the wide open country to come.

"'Save a Horse (Ride a Cowboy)' freaked people out. They went, 'What is *that*?'" Rich said of the single's debut. "Then, ten years later, you hear where country music is now and how it has changed sonically and lyrically—country has never been this wide."

"All I knew was that I hadn't fallen down the stairs, Tim and Faith were hugging me, and those three minutes had become something I would always remember."
—**TAYLOR SWIFT**

Swift was only seventeen when she debuted on the 2007 ACM Awards with her first single, "Tim McGraw," in a bold performance that would foreshadow her future blockbuster live shows. Standing center stage alone with only her guitar, she sang the song, then walked down into the audience to meet Tim for the first time on live national TV.

"In that moment, I didn't look up to realize that every person in the audience was standing up," Swift recalled later for *ACM Tempo*, the Academy's magazine. "I didn't know that then. All I knew was that I hadn't fallen down the stairs, Tim and Faith were hugging me, and those three minutes had become something I would always remember."

The next year Swift would be named the ACM Top New Female Vocalist, and by decade's end she would collect three more trophies, including the prestigious Album of the Year. Although breakthrough female artists were few and far between, the women who did break through were making their mark. Both Lambert and Underwood also won Album of the Year, a category traditionally dominated by the guys. Sugarland's Nettles won 2007's Song of the Year for "Stay," becoming the first woman since Donna Fargo in 1972 to write an ACM Song of the Year solely by herself. And Underwood would take home the Entertainer of the Year awards for 2008 and 2009, making her the first solo female artist to win Entertainer since Shania Twain in 1999.

ABOVE: *Kenny Chesney and George Strait perform "Shiftwork," 2008.*
RIGHT: *Kenny Chesney fresh from winning ACM Entertainer of the Year, 2008.*
OPPOSITE: *Garth Brooks and Trisha Yearwood, 2008.*

While the girls were killing it, Kenny Chesney was breaking records of his own. After his win for 1997 New Male Vocalist, Chesney became a bona fide superstar in the following decade, selling out stadiums and amassing a loyal and passionate fan following from coast to coast. At the 2008 ACM Awards, he won his fourth straight trophy for Entertainer of the Year, tying Garth Brooks for the most consecutive wins in the category for a solo artist.

"I had already been in the business a long time before I was even nominated for Entertainer, so I was able to watch a lot of people that I really looked up to win," Chesney said. "Even before that, I watched a lot of my heroes win from my couch in my college apartment. So, when I won my first Entertainer trophy, it was surreal. Like a dream. I just remember how excited my band, crew, label, and my whole team was. They were all backstage waiting on me to walk off stage to help me celebrate. It was if they had won, and, in a sense, they did because we all had been swimming upstream getting to that point in this business for a long time together."

HOSTS & LOCATIONS

2000 · Dolly Parton
UNIVERSAL AMPHITHEATRE, HOLLYWOOD, CA

2001 · LeAnn Rimes
UNIVERSAL AMPHITHEATRE, HOLLYWOOD, CA

2002 · Reba McEntire
UNIVERSAL AMPHITHEATRE, HOLLYWOOD, CA

2003 · Reba McEntire
MANDALAY BAY EVENTS CENTER, LAS VEGAS, NV

2004 · Reba McEntire
MANDALAY BAY EVENTS CENTER, LAS VEGAS, NV

2005 · No Host
MANDALAY BAY EVENTS CENTER, LAS VEGAS, NV

2006 · Reba McEntire
MGM GRAND GARDEN ARENA, LAS VEGAS, NV

2007 · Reba McEntire
MGM GRAND GARDEN ARENA, LAS VEGAS, NV

2008 · Reba McEntire
MGM GRAND GARDEN ARENA, LAS VEGAS, NV

2009 · Reba McEntire
MGM GRAND GARDEN ARENA, LAS VEGAS, NV

OPPOSITE: *Reba McEntire hosts, 2009.*

LEFT: *Kenny Chesney performs.*

THE ACMs GO DIGITAL

Chesney's fourth win came in the wake of the ACM board of directors opening up Entertainer of the Year voting to fans for the first time, a move championed by new Academy CEO Bob Romeo. Only the third executive officer in the organization's history, Romeo was hired in 2003 and brought with him hard-won lessons from his family's Omaha-based talent promotion business, Romeo Entertainment, as well as twenty years of experience on the ACM board of directors. Romeo took the helm at a time when the digital revolution was bringing big changes to the music industry and the world at large. Through online sites like iTunes and budding social media platforms such as Facebook and, later, Twitter, the masses could access music and communicate with one another in real time. Fans were able to participate with their favorite artists and shows in a way they never had before.

"When successful shows like *American Idol* and *Dancing with the Stars* reached out to their audience the way they did by letting them vote on the winners, I knew that was the future," reflected Romeo. "After that, fans weren't going to be content to just be spectators, they wanted to participate. Our board had the foresight to get ahead of

OPPOSITE: *Brad Paisley, 2008.*
TOP: *ACM CEO Bob Romeo, George Strait, and Garth Brooks, 2009.*
MIDDLE: *Kenny Chesney (middle) with Rac Clark and Dick Clark, 2001.*
BOTTOM: *Celebrating Hillary Scott's birthday are Lady Antebellum bandmates Dave Haywood and Charles Kelley with dick clark productions' Orly Adelson, ACM's Bob Romeo, and CBS' Jack Sussman.*

that curve. We wanted to reach out and touch the fans and make them a part of the show."

Romeo and the board of directors had a vision to expand the franchise, and Las Vegas gave them the perfect place to do just that. In addition to the awards show, the Academy staged free country concerts, created a charity motorcycle ride, and moved both the All-Star Jam after-party and the charity golf tournament to Sin City, creating "The Week Vegas Goes Country®." The ACM Charitable Fund—long the funnel for the Academy's charitable giving—was rebranded as ACM Lifting Lives, giving the Academy a new purpose and mission: lifting lives through the power of music.

"I think the combination of Bob Romeo and Gayle Holcomb made the Academy of Country Music explode," said Rac Clark. "They brought a business sensibility to the organization. They knew what everyone wanted and what would help this franchise, and I think the combination of the two of them and moving to Vegas set us on a path that we are never going to turn back on."

OPPOSITE: *Keith Urban, 2009.*
TOP: *Trace Adkins performs "Honky Tonk Badonkadonk," 2006.*
LEFT: *Hank Williams Jr. teaches friend Kid Rock that you can't say the "F Word" in country music, 2002.*
ABOVE: *Sara Evans performs.*

As the digital decade brought change upon change to the country music community, one constant was clear: George Strait. By 2009, Strait had won nineteen ACM Awards and charted fifty-seven number one hits. That steady recipe of recording great songs and playing to packed arenas earned Strait the Academy's Artist of the Decade award.

"Throughout my career, I've won some very special awards, and I don't take any of them for granted," Strait said during a rare interview on his San Antonio ranch. "But to be getting ACM Artist of the Decade—there's just four other artists who have ever gotten it, and each one of those artists is huge. To be in that company, it's pretty humbling."

Shortly after collecting his trophy during the *George Strait: ACM Artist of the Decade* network special that aired on CBS, Strait played the first concert in the brand-new, state-of-the-art Cowboys Stadium (which would later be renamed AT&T Stadium) in Arlington, Texas. Strait's beloved home state and another cowboy—Dallas Cowboys' owner Jerry Jones—would soon be playing a vital role in helping the ACM Awards celebrate a major milestone.

OPPOSITE TOP LEFT: *Dierks Bentley prepares backstage, 2009.*
OPPOSITE TOP RIGHT: *Actor Jamie Foxx performs George Strait's "You Look So Good in Love," 2009.*
OPPOSITE BOTTOM: *ACM Award winners Jamey Johnson and Lee Ann Womack perform "Give It Away," 2009.*
TOP: *The all-star finale for George Strait: ACM Artist of the Decade, 2009.*
MIDDLE: *John Rich salutes the King.*
BOTTOM: *Garth Brooks presents the Artist of the Decade Award to George Strait, 2009.*

ARTIST OF THE DECADE
GEORGE STRAIT

really don't remember what went through my mind when my name was called each time I won an ACM award over the years except how thrilled I was to win. Most of it is just a blur to me. There is always an exciting vibe going on at those shows. Everybody's nervous, antsy, thinking about their performance, and trying to visit at the same time. It's pretty hectic.

I loved the years with Dick Clark. He is an icon, and I'm proud to have known him personally. He was a great person, but firm in his approach to the show. I can't imagine trying to put all of that together, but he did it with what seemed like ease. He got a little upset with me once when, due to circumstances beyond my control,

I was ten minutes late for rehearsal. I was cohosting the show, which made it even worse. He got over it, but I was totally embarrassed because I hate to be late for anything.

When they gave me the ACM Artist of the Decade award, it was an incredible night for me and my family. It's so humbling to have all of these great artists—who you feel lucky to call your friends—come pay tribute to your career. I want to thank them again for that.

I'll never take for granted all of the times I was invited to, sang at, and actually won some awards at the ACMs. Those nights will always be special in my mind.

—GEORGE STRAIT

OPPOSITE: *George Strait performs.*
ABOVE: *Ronnie Dunn, Jack Ingram, Lee Ann Womack and Kix Brooks celebrate George Strait, 2009.*

ACM Entertainer
of the Year Winners

2000
DIXIE CHICKS

2001
BROOKS & DUNN

2002
TOBY KEITH

2003
TOBY KEITH

2004
KENNY CHESNEY

2005
KENNY CHESNEY

2006
KENNY CHESNEY

2007
KENNY CHESNEY

2008
CARRIE UNDERWOOD

2009
CARRIE UNDERWOOD

LEFT: *Carrie Underwood in the infamous red couture dress, 2009.*

2010+

2010+

There's nothing Reba McEntire can't do. Singer, actress, Broadway star, clothing designer—she has conquered anything she has attempted with class and grace. Her timeless beauty, talent, and never-ending sass made her a go-to host for the ACM Awards over the course of three decades, beginning with her first turn in 1986. In 2010, she was once again helming the show

known as Country Music's Party of the Year® at the MGM Grand Garden Arena in Las Vegas. And just like Reba, who was always growing and tackling new things, the Academy of Country Music had some big changes and exciting surprises in store—including a move east to a bigger venue.

As the new decade kicked off, a staple of the ACM Awards broadcasts, Brooks & Dunn, called it quits after twenty years as a duo. Kix Brooks and Ronnie Dunn let the fans decide which song they'd sing as their final ACM Awards performance ("My Maria" won), and they walked to the podium one last time together to accept ACM Vocal Duo of the Year—their twenty-seventh ACM Award, making them the most awarded artists in Academy history. The pair was toasted the next night by an all-star lineup of their friends on the *ACM Presents: Brooks & Dunn—The Last Rodeo* concert special.

"To think the best in our business thought enough of us to do that was extremely humbling," Brooks said. "I have a copy, but can't bring myself to watch. It's almost embarrassing, if that makes any sense. One day I will! It was a night I'll never forget."

As Kix and Ronnie were riding into the sunset as a duo, yet another new generation of superstars was coming into its own. While Carrie Underwood, Lady Antebellum, and Miranda Lambert first took the ACM stage in the 2000s, they each earned multiple ACM trophies as the new decade opened. Underwood won her second straight trophy for Entertainer of the Year, making her the first woman ever to repeat in that top category.

"I can't wait 'til the day, which I hope is in the very near future, where having females in the category is no big deal whatsoever," Underwood told reporters backstage. "I accept that award on behalf of myself and my fans, but I also think I accept it on behalf of all the other women who came before me who kicked butt and never got the recognition that they deserved."

For Lady Antebellum's Hillary Scott, it truly was a generational shift. She had first attended the ACM Awards in 1996 at Los Angeles' Universal Amphitheater with her mother, ACM nominee Linda Davis, who famously

P. 168: *Miranda Lambert performs, 2014.*
ABOVE: *Reba hosts, 2010.*
OPPOSITE: *Brooks and Dunn during* The Last Rodeo *special, 2010.*

ABOVE: *Lady Antebellum get comfortable at the All-Star Jam, 2010.*
RIGHT: *Ten-year-old Hillary Scott with her parents, Linda Davis and Lang Scott, at the ACM Awards in 1996.*
OPPOSITE TOP: *Blake Shelton, Dierks Bentley, Lady Antebellum and actor Josh Dumel, backstage, 2010.*
OPPOSITE BOTTOM: *Miranda Lambert wins ACM Female Vocalist in 2011.*

dueted with Reba McEntire on "Does He Love You." Just over a decade later, Hillary and her bandmates, Charles Kelley and Dave Haywood, were named ACM Top New Vocal Duo or Group for 2007 and had huge crossover success with the hit single "Need You Now," taking home Song, Single Record, and Vocal Group of the Year at the 2010 show.

"I knew I had some really big shoes to fill with her as my mother, and I always wanted to make her proud, but I never wanted to ride her coattails," Hillary said. "So, to be able to walk on the red carpet with us as a band and experience the ACMs, I felt very proud and truly humbled. Who would have thought looking back on who I was [in 1996], going, 'I'll be here again!' Because, you don't know if that's going to happen, but it's really cool to be."

Charles Kelley's favorite ACM moments have included some encounters with the artists he considers his heroes. "I remember one time meeting George Strait, and maybe I had just had

"I did grow up watching the ACMs as a kid, so to end up standing on that stage accepting an award is a very surreal experience."
—MIRANDA LAMBERT

too much to drink, but I told him we should be best friends," Kelley remembered with a laugh. "I said, 'George, I think we should be best friends.' He goes, 'I'd like that.' He was obviously kidding with me. You're always wondering growing up watching the ACMs, 'What are they like in person?' That was the coolest moment, meeting your heroes and having them be so real."

Lambert, who shares Kelley's respect of her musical heroes, had been named Top New Female Vocalist for 2006 and won Album of the Year for 2007. In the new decade, she continued making music on her terms and finding great support from both country radio and the country music industry. With tales of headstrong women and small-town trials, Lambert is a throwback to spitfire Loretta Lynn, but with a more country rock edge. Songs like "Gunpowder and Lead" and "Mama's Broken Heart" struck a chord with both men and women alike. She won the prestigious Album of the Year category three times in five years, also scoring Single Record and Song of the Year for the reflective ballad "The House That Built Me." She is also the reigning Female Vocalist of the Year, with five trophies—a record in the category for consecutive wins (Reba holds the record for most overall wins with 7).

"It's difficult to choose which moment is more special than the next, because at that moment, what you are experiencing is very special," Lambert said of her many ACM triumphs. "I did grow up watching the ACMs as a kid, so to end up standing on that stage accepting an award for the music you have made is a very surreal experience."

NEW INFLUENCES

Today's country is wide open, giving room for different sounds, influences, and collaborations. Jason Aldean, who first broke through with country rockers like "Hicktown" and "Johnny Cash," combined country with rap on "Dirt Road Anthem," growing his audience and becoming the first country act to play Boston's historic Fenway Park.

ACM Award-winner Dierks Bentley has successfully mixed his love of country and bluegrass, gaining fans among his fellow country artists as well as rockers like U2's Bono. "My first couple of years in the industry were such a blur, but winning my first ACM Award stands out," Bentley said. "I was backstage with my band and crew, and my Mom and Dad walked in, and I had no idea how they snuck their way past security, but they did and they were just so happy. My Dad has since passed away, but I have a great picture of them with huge smiles on their faces."

Eric Church has emerged as a critically acclaimed singer and songwriter, reviving the "outlaw" attitude and recording a wide berth of hits, from the revved up "Smoke a Little Smoke" and the quiet contemplation of "Springsteen" to the simmering intensity of "Give Me Back My Hometown."

"Though I have never made records to win awards, it's always awesome that your peers in the industry recognize your work," said Church, a three-time ACM Award winner. "I think the ACMs are a crucial aspect to the history of country music, whether it be performaces, awards, collaborations or just magical moments. They have helped define the music we make."

Former pop star Darius Rucker, who first found fame as lead singer of Hootie & the Blowfish, made a successful move to country music as a solo act. His number one hit, "Don't Think I Don't Think About It," made him the first African-American to have a chart-topping country song since Charley Pride in 1983.

New artists Kacey Musgraves, The Band Perry, Lee Brice, Justin Moore, Thompson Square, Eli Young Band, Brantley Gilbert, Chris Young, Hunter Hayes, and Florida Georgia Line have also burst onto the scene, each bringing their own interpretation of contemporary country music. Florida Georgia Line—composed of friends Tyler Hubbard and Brian Kelley—came on full force with a mash-up of country and hip hop, sailing through the door first opened by Big & Rich a decade earlier and landing a massive hit with the irresistible "Cruise" and an ACM Award nomination for Vocal Event of the Year with rapper Nelly for the remix version.

"It's just been incredible for what's happening in country music right now. It's just a really cool time for a lot of different sounds, a lot of different artists—younger and older—and collaborations," said Florida Georgia Line's Brian Kelley. "People try to argue about what country music is and what it's going to be and what it was, but to me, it's always been pretty simple. It's about good times and real life experiences and good people, trucks and girls and beer and late nights, early mornings working hard—it's a certain lifestyle."

Pp. 174–175: *Zac Brown & James Taylor, 2011.*
BELOW: *Florida Georgia Line & Nelly, 2013.*
OPPOSITE: *Jason Aldean, 2014.*

TOP: *Rocker Eric Church, 2011.*
ABOVE: *Lee Brice Performs, 2014.*
ABOVE MIDDLE: *Eli Young Band, 2013.*
RIGHT AND OPPOSITE: *Brad Paisley takes a plunge on camera, 2010.*

Hayes, a child prodigy who first started publicly performing at four years old in his native Louisiana, displayed his myriad musical skills, playing every instrument on his debut album and hitting the charts with self-penned songs "Wanted" and "Everybody's Got Somebody But Me." He continued bringing younger fans to the country music, blurring the lines for an audience whose iTunes playlists aren't divided by genres.

No one was more suited to be the face of the new generation of country artists than Blake Shelton, a talented and lovable smartass. A stone country fan with an encyclopedic knowledge of the genre, Shelton is also a fan of music in general and brings that sensibility to his own songs, even cutting the contemporary Christian hit "God Gave Me You" to great acclaim on country radio right alongside his more country-leaning tunes "Honey Bee" and "Boys 'Round Here." Shelton introduced his joie de vivre attitude to the world in 2011 as a judge

on the incredibly popular reality singing competition *The Voice*. He was an instant hit, showing the rest of America what country fans had known and loved all along. Blake joined Reba as cohost of the ACM Awards that same year, proving the perfect partner for the redheaded wonder's comic timing.

"For some reason, we both have a unique personality that, for me, when I get around Blake, it just seems to come out a little bit more," Reba explained. "There's not as [ ] gates that come up. It's all 'what [ ] you get,' and that's what I've [ ] around Blake. He's such a lovable [ ]

One of the hosting duo's f [ ] was making a mad dash duri [ ] cial break through the Vegas St [ ] to the first ever ACM Fan Jam [ ] Mandalay Bay Events Center. Th [ ] show was selling out in minute [ ] Grand, and CEO Bob Romeo so [ ] invite more fans to the party. [ ] was born. Billed as a full-blow [ ] live remotes into the ACM Awa [ ] the Fan Jam gave attendees a [ ]

OPPOSITE TOP: *Hunter Hayes at the ACM Party for a Cause Festival, 2013.*
OPPOSITE BOTTOM: *ACM hosts Blake Shelton and Reba McEntire, 2011.*
TOP: *Reba and Blake huddle with ACM Awards Producer and Writer Barry Adelman, 2011.*
LEFT: *Reba with singer Jennifer Hudson, 2009.*

HOSTS & LOCATIONS

2010 · Reba McEntire
MGM GRAND GARDEN ARENA, LAS VEGAS, NV

2011 · Reba McEntire & Blake Shelton
MGM GRAND GARDEN ARENA, LAS VEGAS, NV

2012 · Reba McEntire & Blake Shelton
MGM GRAND GARDEN ARENA, LAS VEGAS, NV

2013 · Blake Shelton & Luke Bryan
MGM GRAND GARDEN ARENA, LAS VEGAS, NV

2014 · Blake Shelton & Luke Bryan
MGM GRAND GARDEN ARENA, LAS VEGAS, NV

2015 · Blake Shelton & Luke Bryan
AT&T STADIUM, ARLINGTON, TX

OPPOSITE: *Blake Shelton and Luke Bryan hosting, 2014.*
ABOVE: *Blake and Luke take a selfie, 2014.*

> "I think introducing artists from another genre to country music fans is one of the best reveals you'll ever see."
> —SUGARLAND'S KRISTIAN BUSH

up-close-and-personal awards show experience. The Academy was now selling out the two biggest venues on the Vegas Strip.

"We wanted to reach out and touch fans and make them feel like they were actually part of the show," Romeo said. "The ACM Fan Jam was created just for them, and they filled the Mandalay Bay to the rafters that first year. The energy in that room was unbelievable."

Sugarland signed on to host the first Fan Jam, bringing along their full-scale tour production and special guest Rihanna. The pop and R & B star performed her own song, "California King Bed," with Sugarland's Jennifer Nettles, who accepted the ACM Vocal Duo of the Year trophy with partner Kristian Bush while standing in the middle of the fans on the arena floor. Nettles and Bush, like many of today's country acts, are self-described fans of all genres of music, drawing inspiration from a wide variety of influences.

"Rihanna is such an amazing performer," Bush said. "I think introducing artists from another genre to country fans is one of the best reveals you'll ever see, because the guest artists are so delighted that these people are just voracious for them." ACM Fan Jam was so successful the franchise has continued with hosts Zac Brown Band, Brad Paisley, and Florida Georgia Line.

OPPOSITE: *Sugarland host ACM Fan Jam, 2011.*
ABOVE: *Jennifer Nettles duets with Rihanna, 2011.*
LEFT: *Brad Paisley joins the Zac Brown Band for ACM Fan Jam, 2012.*

HOLLYWOOD COUNTRY

Harkening back to the Academy's earliest days, the ACM Awards became a cavalcade of celebrities—both musical and otherwise—coming to join the party. CBS stars Beth Behrs, LL Cool J, and Ashton Kutcher as well as movie stars Robert Pattinson, Reese Witherspoon, Olivia Munn, Liam Hemsworth, Jamie Foxx, and Matthew McConaughey are among those who have served as presenters in recent years.

McConaughey, in particular, provided some comic relief while presenting Male Vocalist of the Year to Brad Paisley. Before announcing the winner, he shared a little too much about his visit to the ACM Awards the year before.

"After the show last year, me and my lady, Camilla, went back to the hotel and conceived the little lady who is now our daughter, Vida Alves McConaughey," he said from the stage as Camilla laughed from her seat in the audience. "That's a true story. We're going to try to *not* get so lucky this year!"

TOP: *Robert Pattinson and Reese Witherspoon, 2011.*
MIDDLE: *Actor Liam Hemsworth presents, 2012.*
BELOW: *Miranda Lambert hangs with future Academy Award-winner Matthew McConaughey, 2011.*
OPPOSITE: *Carrie Underwood duets with rocker Steven Tyler on "Walk This Way," 2011.*

Along with Hollywood's brightest, the decade has seen an amazing list of artists in other genres joining forces with country's biggest stars for some memorable ACM collaborations, including John Fogerty, James Taylor, John Mayer, Steven Tyler, Steve Martin, KISS, Shakira, Stevie Nicks, and Stevie Wonder. This mosaic of talented musicians has also been a staple of some stellar "ACM Presents" TV specials, including *George Strait—Artist of the Decade, Brooks & Dunn—The Last Rodeo, Girls' Night Out—Superstar Women of Country, Lionel Richie and Friends, Tim McGraw's Superstar Summer Night,* and *An All-Star Salute to the Troops—* which all benefitted the Academy's charitable arm, ACM Lifting Lives. The magic combination of great songs you know and love sung by unexpected artists has been a winner, giving country fans something new and fresh each time.

ABOVE: *Reba and Kelly Clarkson hang with KISS backstage, 2012.*
OPPOSITE: *Jennifer Nettles, Miranda Lambert, Reba McEntire, Martina McBride, Carrie Underwood, and The Judds are feted at* ACM Presents: Girls' Night Out.

"I still can't believe that we pulled that performance off! We knew it had to be kept secret in order to have the maximum impact . . . we just wanted to surprise everyone. And we did! I had so much fun up there with Steven, and even now, I will pull up that YouTube video to watch again."

—CARRIE UNDERWOOD

TOP: *Taylor Swift crowd surfing, 2010.*
ABOVE: *Taylor Swift reacts to her first ACM Entertainer of the Year win with mom Andrea, 2011.*
OPPOSITE: *Taylor Swift performs "Should've Said No."*

TAYLOR NATION

A common face at many of these ACM specials and the ACM Awards stage alike was phenomenon Taylor Swift, whose star rose in an unprecedented fashion and continues to take country music to places never dreamed. Winning ACM Top New Female Vocalist for 2007, she became, only one year later, the top-selling artist in all genres of music, earning the ACM Crystal Milestone Award for this amazing feat in 2008. It's impossible to catalog Swift's many accolades both as a singer and a songwriter, but her self-penned tunes, "Our Song," "Mean," "I Knew You Were Trouble," and "We Are Never Ever Getting Back Together," bonded her with fans across the globe, bringing her multiplatinum album sales, sold-out tours, and more trophies than she could count. Swift's penchant for writing songs from her own experiences, including past relationships, is now legendary. Her willingness to ex-

periment with different sounds on her albums, from the fun pop of "22" to the stripped-down emotion of "Begin Again," made her a hit on both the country and pop charts and gave her an endless canvas for her dynamic live shows, which she took to Australia, Europe, and Asia. On the ACM Awards, Swift worked with show producers Rac Clark and Barry Adelman to stage one-of-a-kind performances of her songs, whether dancing in the rain, flying over the crowd, or appearing out of thin air thanks to magician David Copperfield.

"With every performance, I've gotten to do something new on the ACMs, and I've always loved that about that awards show," Swift said. "A real career changer for me was when I performed 'Should've Said No,' and then got completely soaked by all this water onstage. That memory is one that I'll always think back on and smile, because the ACMs have always let me really, really stretch my ideas into something that turned out to be creative and fun."

Her tenacity both onstage and in her writing paid off in spades as fans voted her ACM Entertainer of the Year for both 2010 and 2011.

"All I remember about winning Entertainer of the Year is pure joy, overwhelming panic, and a rush of emotion I can't even describe," Swift said. "Having watched the ACMs every year since I was little, it's the most insane feeling to actually walk up there and receive that huge award. It awards everyone you work with, your touring family, the people who helped you create the album, and your fans."

SO LONG, DICK

The same year that Taylor was taking country to new heights by breaking down musical barriers, the music industry lost a tireless supporter who had spent his whole professional career doing that very thing. TV icon Dick Clark, who had shepherded the Academy of Country Music Awards into a national network franchise, died on April 18, 2012, at the age of eighty-two in Santa Monica, California. The last awards show he attended was the ACM Awards, where he watched from his Las Vegas hotel suite.

"The final performance was a duet by Blake Shelton and Lionel Richie," Dick's longtime friend and colleague Barry Adelman said. "Few in attendance, or viewing at home, knew the irony of the moment. Lionel Richie's first ever appearance on television was in 1976 as the lead singer of the Commodores . . . on *American Bandstand*. What must Dick have been thinking as he watched so many of his worlds, professionally, personally, and musically, come together in one moment with his son producing it all?"

During the 2013 ACM Awards, at the personal invitation of Rac Clark, George Strait and Garth Brooks performed together for the first time in memory of Dick. It was a fitting tribute, as both winners of the ACM Artist of the Decade performed after Reba announced that the Academy's board of directors had voted to rename the award the ACM Dick Clark Artist of the Decade Award.

"I always needed to be on time to a Dick Clark production because I knew Dick would be waiting," Reba said. "Sometimes when I was hosting the ACMs, when we were waiting onstage for the next event to take place, we'd take pictures, tell stories, and simply enjoy the moment. I enjoyed being around Dick. Our sensibilities were very similar. We loved our jobs and the people we got to work with."

BELOW: *Blake Shelton performs with Lionel Richie, 2012.*
OPPOSITE TOP: *"Bluke" is born, 2013.*
OPPOSITE BOTTOM: *Hosts Blake Shelton and Luke Bryan share an off-stage moment, 2013.*

#BLUKE

After walking onto the ACM Awards stage a record fourteen times as host, Reba decided to step down in 2013 to focus her energies on other creative projects. She handed the microphone to Luke Bryan, who joined his buddy Blake Shelton as co-host. With smash hits "Drunk on You" and "Crash My Party," Bryan soared to headliner status with his catchy songs and sweet Georgia-boy charm. His dance moves onstage earned him a devoted female following, and his perpetual smile and ready sense of humor were a great match for Shelton's say-anything attitude, which he continued to put on full display to a national audience on *The Voice*. During a CBS promo shoot in Nashville, the bro-mance name "Bluke" was born, and boy, did it stick. Fans across the country were snapping photos of themselves with their "Flat Blukes" (photos of Blake and Luke that they could print at home), taking the boys to the Grand Canyon and the White House among countless other settings and posting to social networks with the hashtag #Bluke. Blake and Luke took it all in stride and brought their off-stage friendship with them to the stage at the MGM Grand Garden Arena, picking on each other as if they were just sitting around backstage having a beer.

"Know what a Motel 6 and Luke's jeans have in common? No ballroom!" Blake cracked in the opening monologue, clearly having a good time.

> "This is the defining moment of my life, and it means the world to me. I will never take it for granted."
> —LUKE BRYAN

It would prove a good night for both Blake and Luke. In his one serious moment of the night, Blake would accept Song of the Year for "Over You" with his wife, Miranda. The song laid bare the hurt and confusion Blake endured when he lost his older brother, Richie, to a car accident in 1990.

"I've learned so much from this human being standing next to me about myself," Blake said as Miranda clutched her trophy and held back tears. "She blows me away. I used to think I was a decent songwriter until I started hanging around with her, and she really taught me how to write a good song, and this is proof of it."

Miranda had her own words to add about the win. "As a songwriter, having your songs and your lyrics recognized by your peers is pretty much as good as it gets. Thank you for accepting me as a songwriter and not just a singer and performer. That means the world to me."

Luke would walk away the night's big winner. Only three years after winning New Artist of the Year, he heard his name called when Shania Twain announced Entertainer of the Year. Blake enveloped Luke in a big bear hug just off-stage, and the shocked singer took a full minute onscreen to compose himself before he could speak.

"Thank you guys so much, fans, for doing this for me. Thank you for making my life what it is," he told the audience. "What I always wanted to be was just a country singer that got to ride on a tour bus and show up at a new stage and play music every night. Every time I step on stage it is a blessing to me to play for fans. This is the defining moment of my life, and it means the world to me and I will never take it for granted."

BELOW: *Luke Bryan wins ACM Entertainer of the Year in 2013.* OPPOSITE: *Blake Shelton and wife Miranda Lambert share a win for ACM Song of the Year, 2013.*

FIFTY FABULOUS YEARS

More than sixteen million viewers watched the 2013 ACM Awards, and as the network show grew for CBS, so did the Academy's plans for its premier franchise. The Week Vegas Goes Country® had swelled to include the ACM Party for a Cause® Festival, a two-day music festival that spotlighted various deserving charities. And with both the awards show at the MGM Grand and

> "We've always tried to reach out to fans and engage them, and what better way than to invite them to join us at Cowboys Stadium for the largest awards show ever staged?"
> —ACM CEO BOB ROMEO

the Fan Jam at Mandalay Bay selling out, it was time to broaden the scope for the ACM Awards upcoming fiftieth anniversary. The vision had actually started years before, when Academy CEO Bob Romeo had the crazy notion to take the show to Texas to the massive AT&T Stadium—Home of the Dallas Cowboys.

"[Dallas Cowboys' owner] Jerry Jones invited us to come open the stadium in 2009, but it wasn't going to be ready by our show date," Romeo recalls. "But the idea never left me. I knew there was something special there! We've always tried to reach out to fans and engage them, and what better way than to invite them to join us at Cowboys Stadium for the largest awards show ever staged?"

RIGHT: *Faith Hill on* ACM Presents: Tim McGraw's Superstar Summer Night, *2013.*

At the 2014 ACM Awards show on April 6—hosted once again by Blake Shelton and Luke Bryan—the dream became a reality when Jones and Texas-native George Strait walked onto the ACM Awards stage and announced that the show was headed to Dallas for the fiftieth anniversary ACM Awards on April 19, 2015.

"We'll meet you in Texas," Strait told the millions watching at home, just moments before the fans named him ACM Entertainer of the Year.

Backstage shortly after the announcement, Jones said the ACM Awards, Texas, and the Home of the Cowboys are a natural fit.

"They call the Cowboys 'America's Team,' and this is 'America's Music,'" Jones said. "To be able to have the venue that can celebrate the 50th year of these ACM Awards is a privilege."

"It's a daunting task, but it's just the right thing to do to mark our fiftieth anniversary," Romeo said. "We're going to a place that U2 has played, that the Final Four has played, that the Super Bowl has played. To think we could go in there and sell that out to 75,000 fans, what a fabulous statement for country music. I think this will be an experience that will be unbelievable not only for us, but for the fans and the country artists themselves."

Tickets for both the 50th ACM Awards and ACM Party for a Cause—a two-day outdoor concert at Globe Life Park (Home of the Texas Rangers)—went on sale on April 15, 2014. They sold out in 18 minutes, setting the stage for one hell of a party.

From the Red Barrel Niteclub in 1963 to AT&T Stadium in 2015, it's still Country Music's Party of the Year®, and everyone is invited.

OPPOSITE TOP: *Jerry Jones and George Strait, 2014.*
OPPOSITE BOTTOM: *George Strait shares his Entertainer of the Year win with Taylor Swift and his wife, Norma, 2014.*
TOP: *George Strait, Garth Brooks, and Miranda Lambert honor Merle Haggard's fifty years in country music with the ACM Crystal Milestone Award, 2014.*
LEFT: *Kacey Musgraves wins ACM Album of the Year, 2014.*

ABOVE: *Luke Bryan, 2014.*
OPPOSITE: *ACM New Artist of the Year Justin Moore plays the ACM Party for a Cause Festival at The Linq, 2014.*

ACM Entertainer
of the Year Winners

2010
TAYLOR SWIFT

2011
TAYLOR SWIFT

2012
LUKE BRYAN

2013
GEORGE STRAIT

Trophies are presented to honor music from the previous calendar year.

LEFT: *Tim McGraw, Keith Urban, and Taylor Swift perform "Highway Don't Care," 2013.*
ABOVE: *Taylor meets the fans, 2014.*

BLAKE SHELTON

Growing up in Oklahoma, my family and I always watched the ACM Awards every year. I am the biggest country music fan on the planet, and this show had the biggest stars from the radio in one place singing all the songs I loved. When I watched as a kid, I always wondered how hard it was for the people who hosted the show to remember the monologue. Now I know exactly how hard it is. Thanks, Rac!

The year I was tapped to host the show with my amazing friend and mentor Reba is seared in my brain. The moment that sticks with me most is the second before Reba and I were getting ready to walk onstage at the MGM Grand Garden Arena. Cher—yes, *the* Cher—was introducing us, and I thought I was going to faint. This was before I invited Cher to be a mentor for my team on *The Voice,* so it was like meeting musical royalty.

Thankfully, I didn't pass out, and I made it through the show well enough that they've had me back every year since.

After two great years with Reba, they paired me with this yahoo named Luke Bryan. Ever heard of him? The guy dances at the drop of a hat and can't quit smiling, but I guess he's as good a cohost as any. Seriously, Luke's a great guy, and we've had fun trying to give the CBS censors a heart attack every April.

I love to be a part of the ACMs in any way I can, whether it was back in the old days with a performance or a presenter's slot or just to be in the audience. But to have the opportunity to be on that stage and be the voice of the ACMs for the night, it's just an honor. You would have to be crazy not to jump at that opportunity, and I can't imagine not doing it now that I've done it for a couple of years. It's so much fun, and my favorite thing about it probably is during the monologue just to look down in the audience and see the looks on all the artists' faces down there, just the fear of, "Oh my God, please don't talk about the pictures that just came out of me or some story that just broke." You can tell that they're all just out there sweating it out. I'm kinda sweating it out, too. It's one thing to be funny when you're sitting in a restaurant with somebody, but it's another thing whenever people expect it and you end up getting a gig because of it.

The first ACM Award I ever won was with Trace Adkins for Vocal Event of the Year for "Hillbilly Bone," but they didn't give it to us on camera; they surprised us with it the night

before the show. They made up for it a couple of years later though, when I got to stand on stage in front of my friends and the whole country to accept ACM Male Vocalist of the Year. It took me ten years to win that trophy. But the ACM Award that means the most to me is the Song of the Year trophy that I won with Miranda. I've never been really confident in my songwriting skills, but "Over You" came from a very raw and honest place in my heart. Winning ACM Song of the Year is still the most important moment to me in my career.

After fifty years, the ACM Awards is still an important event, not only because it recognizes the accomplishments of our established artists, but also because, historically, it has been the only awards show to take chances on new artists and allow them to perform in front of millions of people. That's the only way new artists can become superstars, and it's the only way country music will thrive for that new generation that's now watching the ACM Awards at home, just like I did. Here's to another fifty years of great country music television moments—especially ones that have me in them!

—BLAKE SHELTON

TOP: *Blake and Miranda, 2011.*
OPPOSITE: *Blake performs, 2012.*

LUKE BRYAN

The overall vibe of the ACM Awards backstage can be summed up in two words: Vegas and fun. It's just a real positive feeling. Backstage, everybody is having the time of their lives, getting ready to perform. People are moving the set pieces in and out. It's a fun place to be. Hosting the ACM Awards was a huge dream come true for me. I've been a fan of country music for as long as I can remember, and finding myself onstage hosting such an important awards show and being a

part of that role was very overwhelming for me. Being up there with Blake—knowing that people were going to be laughing with us and knowing that it was just going to be a fun night for country music—I was so proud to be a part of that night, and I was so thankful to be asked to be a host. Blake is such a cut-up, but when it was time to be serious, it was amazing to watch him. It's cool when you see somebody as a true professional and it inspires you to be the same and that's obviously what Blake Shelton is.

I was named ACM Top New Artist of the Year for 2009, and it was my first major award. I remember thinking this was all I ever could have dreamed of at that moment, and I will be forever proud to say that for that year, I was the best new artist. It's something that still brings a smile to my face when I think about those moments. But my most vivid memory of the ACM Awards definitely was winning Entertainer of the Year in 2013. When Shania announced the winner, I was backstage with Blake, and I remember him picking me up and doing the whole bear hug thing and squeezing the breath out of me. The overall emotion that I shared being in that room and being onstage and being a part of that moment is still something that I think about every day and I can't believe that it happened to me. Right afterward Jason Aldean ran up on the stage and gave me a big hug and a high five, and my buddy Dallas Davidson did, too. And then I got to see my family right after that happened—my wife, Caroline, and my parents—and it was a truly life-changing experience. I don't talk about it a lot, but I've lost both my brother and my sister. Our family has dealt with a lot of tragedy, so that night was just a positive moment that we could share together. You know they're in Heaven smiling down on moments like this.

When I think of all the artists at the ACM Awards, I realize that I've really seen everybody there over the years.

I've seen the legends, the heroes, the Garths, the Alans, the Georges of the world, and the Alabamas. And they've brought in amazing guests through the years. I've watched artists like Miranda and Blake blossom into superstars on that stage. I've always really enjoyed watching Miranda win awards because she's so heartfelt and truly appreciative. When I think about the ACMs being fifty years old, I think about the show being a staple on my TV as a kid and watching my heroes—Dolly Parton and Kenny Rogers and Ronnie Milsap—perform on that stage and me sitting in the living room. It was one of the nights of the year when we got to eat supper in the den and watch the ACM Awards and see how they've evolved with country music through the years. They've helped artists grow their career and given artists the chance to win awards and be onstage and become bigger, more important country artists and even mainstream artists. So, it's been an amazing fifty years and I'm certainly proud to say that I have left my own small mark on that fifty years and hopefully I'll be around when the next fifty rolls by.

–LUKE BRYAN

OPPOSITE: *Luke performs, 2013.*
TOP: *Luke interacts with the fans, 2013.*

ACM
LIFTING LIVES

ACM LIFTING LIVES

Carrie Underwood stood smiling on the edge of the auditorium stage, hidden from the crowd by a dark curtain. Dressed casually in a yellow sundress and boots, she listened as her former elementary school vocal coach introduced her to the chattering students assembled at Checotah High School, her Oklahoma alma mater. Her unannounced appearance wasn't the only surprise of the day, as Carrie had brought along with her shiny new instruments for the school's music department, a much-needed contribution worth more than $100,000.

The donation was made possible in part by Carrie's ACM Entertainer of the Year Matching Grant, which was established by the Academy's charitable arm, ACM Lifting Lives, to honor the artist who wins the top prize at the ACM Awards each year. The idea came from Carrie's own wish to do something great for her community, and the ACM Lifting Lives board of directors decided to make the concept a yearly gift. Carrie was able to choose her favorite cause, and ACM Lifting Lives matched the donation made by her very own C.A.T.S. Foundation.

"ACM Lifting Lives is about making the lives of kids and people better through music, and that's what I want to do, too," Underwood said.

Partnering with generous country artists to give back has always been part of the Academy of Country Music's DNA. Since its inception in the 1960s, the Academy has sponsored celebrity golf tournaments and charitable concerts to raise money for a wide range of deserving organizations like Shriners Hospitals for Children, Wounded Warrior Project, and Folds of Honor.

In 2001, the Academy partnered with The Home Depot to create the ACM/The Home Depot Humanitarian Award, which recognized the generous efforts of country stars like Vince Gill, Reba McEntire, Brooks & Dunn, and Martina McBride. The winners were invited to build a playground in the city of their choice with the help of non-profit powerhouse KaBOOM! Thanks to those efforts, today cities like New Orleans and Shreveport, Louisiana; Medicine Lodge, Kansas; and Jackson, Tennessee, have safe playgrounds for local children to enjoy.

After years of being called the ACM Charitable Fund, the Academy's philanthropic arm was reborn as ACM Lifting Lives in 2009. The new mission of "improving lives through the power of music" was quickly embraced by artists like two-time ACM Entertainer of the Year Underwood and ACM Award winners Trace Adkins and Toby

P. 208: *Darius Rucker with the ACM Lifting Lives Music Campers, 2010.*
ABOVE: *Carrie Underwood, 2009.*
OPPOSITE: *Brett Eldredge at ACM Lifting Lives Music Camp, 2012.*

ABOVE: *Trace Adkins with the West Point Glee Club, 2009.*
OPPOSITE TOP: *Jerrod Niemann with the ACM Lifting Lives Music Campers on the Grand Ole Opry, 2013.*
OPPOSITE BOTTOM: *Little Big Town with camper Gary, 2012.*

Keith, who were among the first onboard. Two-time ACM Entertainer of the Year winner Taylor Swift designated her matching grant money to St. Jude Children's Research Hospital in Memphis, Tennessee, and Luke Bryan donated his grant to Shriners Hospitals for Children. Along with the Entertainer of the Year matching grants, ACM Lifting Lives has also established the "My Cause" web series, which gives artists a platform to promote their favorite charitable causes. In addition, the Diane Holcomb Emergency Relief Fund gives quick assistance to those in the music industry who've been hit by emergency or catastrophic events. To date, ACM Lifting Lives has awarded more than eight million dollars to deserving groups who truly are improving lives through the power of music.

The Academy has also donated valuable primetime TV airtime to some amazing national causes through what is commonly called the ACM Lifting Lives "show moment" during the annual ACM Awards. The inaugural moment was a chill-inducing performance from Adkins supported by the West Point Glee Club on "'Til the

Last Shot's Fired." The haunting song, told from the perspective of several fallen soldiers, encouraged viewers to think about the warrior, not the war, and supported the Wounded Warrior Project, a nonprofit that aids wounded American veterans and their families. Subsequent ACM Lifting Lives moments have included Keith for Stand Up 2 Cancer and Little Big Town, Jewel, and Hunter Hayes for Child Hunger Ends Here.

In 2011, the show moment spotlighted another ACM Lifting Lives endeavor, the ACM Lifting Lives Music Camp. Held each summer in Nashville in partnership with the Vanderbilt Kennedy Center the camp offers a weeklong, once-in-a-lifetime experience for young adults with Williams syndrome and other developmental delays. Campers from the ages of late teens to early forties travel to Nashville, where they are exposed to experiences any aspiring songwriter or musician would dream of—including writing an original song with the top tunesmiths in Nashville. The 2010 campers crafted a song with artist Chris Young and songwriter Brett James called "Music From the Heart." Capitol Nashville recording artist Darius Rucker joined the campers on the 46th ACM Awards to perform the song live in front of 13.5 million viewers on CBS. Rucker's Southern gospel spin and the campers' unbridled enthusiasm took the song to church, eliciting tears from Underwood and a standing ovation from front-row artists including Keith Urban and Taylor Swift. Those three minutes on national television pointed a positive light toward developmental disabilities and gave the campers a moment in the sun that their families never dared hope for.

To raise funds for the continued work of Lifting Lives, the Academy began staging a series of all-star CBS concert specials in 2009 with proceeds earmarked for the charity.

Launching with *George Strait: ACM Artist of the Decade All Star Concert*, the Academy and producing partner dick clark productions brought together an incredible line-up to honor the artistry of legend George Strait, the Academy's Artist of the Decade for the 2000s. Held the day after the ACM Awards show, the yearly specials have become an anticipated event and subsequent shows under the *ACM Presents* banner have included *Brooks & Dunn—The Last Rodeo*, celebrating the culmination of twenty-seven-time ACM Award winners Brooks & Dunn; *Girls' Night Out: Superstar Women of Country*, which honored the careers of Reba McEntire, Carrie Underwood, Martina McBride, Sugarland's Jennifer Nettles, Miranda Lambert, and the Judds; *Lionel Richie and Friends*, which brought to life Richie's country duets album, *Tuskegee*, and helped it sell more than a million copies; and *Tim McGraw's Superstar Summer Night*, which showcased Tim, his favorite artists, and their most cherished charitable causes. Included in the special was the poignant moment when Tim—through his Operation Homefront program—gave a mortgage-free home to returning soldier Sgt. Mathew Pickard and his family before a live audience at the ACM Party for a Cause® Festival in Las Vegas.

"I've been a part of the ACMs for a long, long time, and they've been with me for a long time," McGraw said of his partnership with ACM Lifting Lives. "They've done fantastic

things for charity throughout the entire association that I've had with them. I thought it was just a perfect match."

By holding this book, you are also improving lives through the power of music. The Academy's proceeds from the sale of this book will go directly to ACM Lifting Lives to help continue its work over the next fifty years.

ABOVE: People *Magazine* An All-Star Salute to the Troops *photoshoot.*

2014: ACM PRESENTS: An All-Star Salute to the Troops. Photographed for *People* magazine on Monday, April 7, 2014. By Gavin Bond

ABOVE: George Strait: Artist of the Decade (2009): *(left to right) Tim McGraw, Faith Hill, Jack Ingram, Taylor Swift, Keith Urban, Martina McBride, Miranda Lambert, Blake Shelton, John Rich (2nd row) Dierks Bentley, Jamey Johnson, Alan Jackson, Lee Ann Womack, George Strait, Jamie Foxx, LeAnn Rimes, Kix Brooks (3rd row) Eddie Montgomery, Troy Gentry, Jennifer Nettles, Kristian Bush, Ronnie Dunn, and Toby Keith.*

ABOVE: ACM Presents: Brooks & Dunn—The Last Rodeo (2010): *(left to right) Tim McGraw, Faith Hill, Kix Brooks, Ronnie Dunn, Reba, Brad Paisley, Carrie Underwood (2nd row) Taylor Swift, Miranda Cosgrove, Keith Urban, Kenny Chesney, Jennifer Hudson, George Strait, Miranda Lambert, Jason Aldean (3rd row) Kristian Bush, Jennifer Nettles, Gary LeVox (4th row) Darius Rucker, Dave Haywood, Hillary Scott, Charles Kelley, Jay DeMarcus, and Joe Don Rooney.*

ABOVE: ACM Presents: Lionel Richie and Friends (2012): (left to right) Kenny Chesney, Martina McBride, Tim McGraw, Darius Rucker, Kenny Rogers, Nicole Richie, Lionel Richie, Luke Bryan, Jennifer Nettles, Marc Anthony (2nd row) Jay DeMarcus, Joe Don Rooney, Gary LeVox, John Rich, Big Kenny, Sara Evans, Jason Aldean, Charles Kelley, Hillary Scott, Dave Haywood (3rd row) Neil Perry, Kimberly Perry and Reid Perry.

ABOVE: ACM Presents: Tim McGraw's Superstar Summer Night (2013): (left to right) Nelly, Taylor Swift, Dierks Bentley, Jason Aldean, Faith Hill, Tim McGraw, Keith Urban, Ne-Yo, Pitbull (2nd row) Reid Perry, Neil Perry, Kimberly Perry, John Fogerty, Luke Bryan, Tyler Hubbard, Brian Kelley, Brantley Gilbert, Charles Kelley, Dave Haywood, and Hillary Scott.

AFTERWORD

Music has always been a sign of the times, and the talented artists who have graced the ACM Awards stage over the past fifty years have been living examples of where we've been, where we are now, and where we are headed as both a genre and a nation. A good country song can make you laugh or cry, inspire you or make you stop and reflect. It can take you back to a special moment, and it can make you dream of those special moments to come. Country music's power is

as strong today as it was back in 1964 when the Academy was founded. And that power is now able to reach fans in ways we could have never imagined.

Today, we live in a digital age that connects the Academy and country music performers to their audience like never before. Fans have been welcomed into the lives and homes of their favorite artists, whether through YouTube, Twitter, or Instagram—and the list goes on. With so much technology at our fingertips, it is no wonder the Academy will continue to embrace the fans in bigger and better ways.

Looking to the future, we want to ensure that the relationship we have with our fans continues to grow deeper with each awards show. We want to continue to open up our world to our fans, and hear what they have to say—about pretty much everything. We've invited them to vote for our Entertainer of the Year and New Artist of the Year awards (expanding the vote to include fans in Canada and Australia, where our show airs live). To keep up with ticket demand, we've added the ACM Fan Jam remote broadcast into the main Awards telecast—an event created just for the fans, so they can be closer to the artists they adore and support out on the road with their hard-earned money.

The success of The Week Vegas Goes Country® led to the ACM Party for a Cause® Festival—a two-day country music festival with ticket proceeds benefitting ACM Lifting Lives and other charities close to our artists' hearts. Fans are now able to connect with artists on an even deeper level, through

both their philanthropic and their musical passions. The mission of our charitable arm, ACM Lifting Lives, is "improving lives through the power of music," and that has truly become the light that guides us. The Academy's board fully embraced that way of thinking, adopting a new mission statement for the entire ACM: "to improve lives by connecting and engaging fans, artists and the industry." It's about more than just ratings or attendance records; it's about giving fans and artists a chance to connect and make a difference.

To celebrate the fiftieth anniversary of the Academy of Country Music Awards in 2015, we're moving the show to one of the biggest and most state-of-the-art venues in the world—AT&T Stadium—the home of the Dallas Cowboys. In the great state of Texas, country music is a way of life, and it is truly a place where any fan can be a part of ACM week and be immersed in the music, the excitement, and the thrill of making history as the largest awards show ever staged.

We're thankful to the fans for helping the Academy get to where we are today. It's impossible to know where another year will take us, but a few things are certain: Country music will continue to dominate; the artists, musicians, and songwriters will continue the good work of those who have helped us build over the past fifty years; and the legacy will continue.

–BOB ROMEO
Chief Executive Officer
The Academy of Country Music

OPPOSITE: *Dierks Bentley and Sheryl Crow perform "I Hold On," 2014.*
TOP: *ACM CEO Bob Romeo.*
P. 220: *Luke Bryan, 2014.*

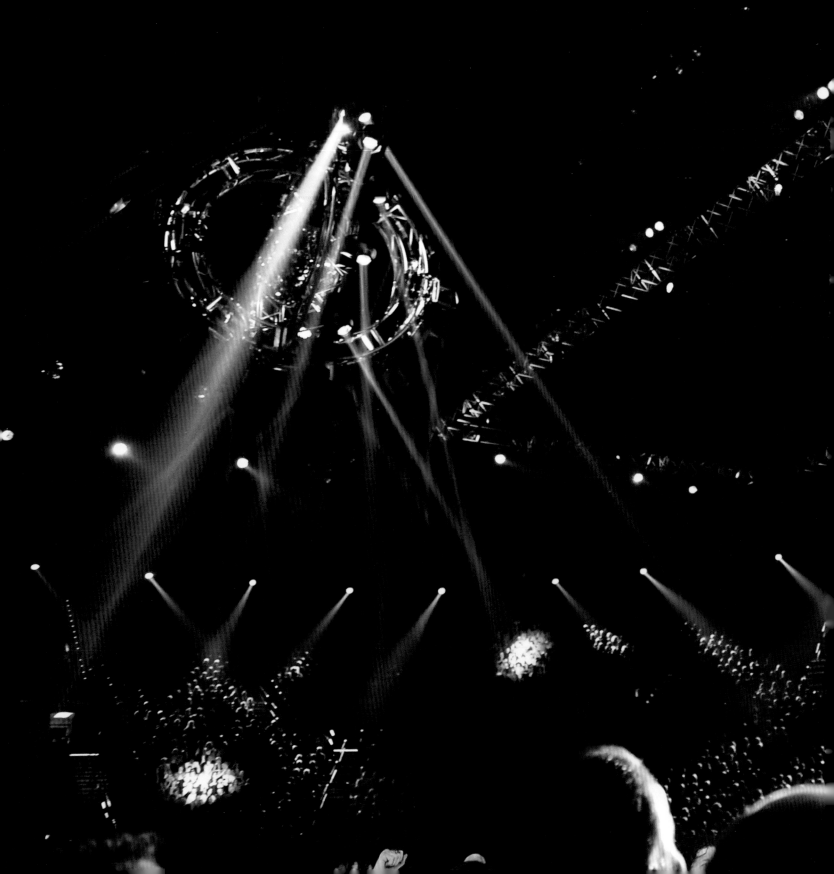

THE ACADEMY OF COUNTRY MUSIC WISHES TO THANK:

Reba McEntire, Marty Stuart, Loretta Lynn, Randy Owen, Garth Brooks, George Strait, Blake Shelton, Luke Bryan, Taylor Swift, Carrie Underwood, Miranda Lambert, Lady Antebellum, Tim McGraw, Faith Hill, Kenny Chesney, Merle Haggard, Dierks Bentley, Dwight Yoakam, Vince Gill, Martina McBride, Kristian Bush, John Rich, Kix Brooks, Ronnie Dunn, Clint Black, Trisha Yearwood, Teddy Gentry, Jeff Cook, Roy Clark, Barbara Mandrell, Charley Pride, Joe Bonsall, Charlie Daniels, Tommy Wiggins, Janet McBride, the late Mickey Christensen, Billy Mize, Joe Saunders, Rac Clark, Barry Adelman, Fran Boyd, Shari Boyd, David Young, Marge Meoli, Jerry Jones, Marion Kraft, Mary Hilliard Harrington, Tresa Redburn, Frank Mull, Justin McIntosh, Dana Lobb, Narvel Blackstock, Brandon Blackstock, Kerri Edwards, Nancy Seltzer, Gayle Holcomb, Pete Fisher, Irv Woolsey, Dottie Oelhafen, Ebie McFarland, Patsy Lynn, Jessie Schmidt, Tree Paine, Paula Erickson, Paul Freundlich, Robert K. Oermann, Wes Vause, Kyle Quiqley, Elaine Schock, Chris and Suzanne Christensen, Don Murray Grubbs, Liz Norris, Greg Gosselin, Bettie Azevedo, Bob Kingsley, Jim Halsey, Kirt Webster , Ron Wolfson, Getty Images, Kevin Winter, Andrew Goodman, dick clark productions; all artists, managers, and publicists who contributed to this book, and to all Academy staff, ACM Board of Directors, members, and volunteers, past and present.

CLOCKWISE FROM TOP LEFT: *The late Mickey Christensen backstage with George Strait at the 2009 ACM Awards; Thompson Square; Jake Owen; Kip Moore; Shawn Parr, Rac Clark and Barry Adelman; Clint Black and Lisa Hartman; Tommy Wiggins winning his ACM Mae Boren Axton Award; Kellie Pickler with Air Force Staff Sgt. Baily Zimmerman on An All-Star Salute to the Troops, 2014; ACM Award–winner Brantley Gilbert, 2013; ACM New Artist of the Year Scotty McCreery, 2012; ACM Award–winners Julianne Hough and Jack Ingram, 2009.*

THE AUTHOR WISHES TO THANK: The amazing artists and photographers who contributed to this project; Tommy Wiggins, the late Mickey Christensen, and Janet McBride; WME's Mel Berger; editor extraordinaire Talia Platz; Robbie Schmidt and the Insight Editions team; our fearless leader, Bob Romeo; Brooke Primero, Lauren Brauchli, Jenny Driessen, Jenelle Scott, Addie Salomon, Teresa George, and Tiffany Moon; and the incredible ACM staffers, both past and present. To Charlie, Faye, and Jason for the roots, and to Doug, Grayson, and Jackson for the wings. AOI

ACM STAFF: Bob Romeo, Tiffany Moon, Teresa George, Lisa Lee, Erick Long, Brooke Primero, Alexa Fasheh, Nichelle Zolezzi, Lauren Brauchli, Amy Cannon, Jenny Driessen, Kate Kramer, Hannah Martin, Tommy Moore, Wes Perry, Addie Salomon, Nick Sammons, Jenelle Scott, Kathryn Nauman, Lindsay Potts, Gentry Alverson, Janet Edbrooke, Taylor Payne, Jon Sands, and Kenzie Todd.

INSIGHT
EDITIONS

PO Box 3088
San Rafael, CA 94912
www.insighteditions.com

Find us on Facebook: www.facebook.com/InsightEditions
Follow us on Twitter: @insighteditions

Library of Congress Cataloging-in-Publication Data available.

ISBN: 978-1-60887-315-9

The Academy's proceeds from this book will go to ACM Lifting Lives to
improve lives through the power of music. www.liftinglives.org

 REPLANTED PAPER   ROOTS of PEACE

Insight Editions, in association with Roots of Peace, will plant two trees for each tree used in the
manufacturing of this book. Roots of Peace is an internationally renowned humanitarian organization
dedicated to eradicating land mines worldwide and converting war-torn lands into productive farms and
wildlife habitats. Roots of Peace will plant two million fruit and nut trees in Afghanistan and provide
farmers there with the skills and support necessary for sustainable land use.

Manufactured in China by Insight Editions

10 9 8 7 6 5 4 3 2 1

INSIGHT EDITIONS

Publisher: Raoul Goff
Co-publisher: Michael Madden
Acquisitions Manager: Robbie Schmidt
Art Director: Chrissy Kwasnik
Book Design: Jenelle Wagner & Chrissy Kwasnik
Book Layout: Jenelle Wagner
Executive Editor: Vanessa Lopez
Project Editor: Talia Platz
Production Manager: Jane Chinn

All photos courtesy of the Academy of Country Music unless
indicated below:

p. 28: Credit: Getty Images. Photo by Michael Ochs Archives

The Academy would like to thank the following individuals for their
contributions to the ACM archives:

1960s & 1970s: Tommy Wiggins, Billy Mize, Janet McBride,
Charles Kruzich, Steve Schatzberg, Chris and Suzanne Christensen

1980s & 1990s: Ron Wolfson, Jasper Dailey

2000s & 2010s: Michael Buckner, Michael Caulfield, Rick
Diamond, Jerod Harris, Frazer Harrison, Frank Micelotta, Ethan
Miller, Christopher Polk, Ed Rode, Kevin Winter, Ron Watson,
Getty Images

ABOVE: *Chris Young performs, 2011.*

ACADEMY OF
COUNTRY MUSIC
★ Awards Dinner ★
UNIVERSAL STUDIOS • HOLLYWOOD
TUESDAY • MAY 3, 1994 • 8:00 PM

UNIVERSAL
AMPHITHEATER
M
MONDAY
APRIL 21, 1997
dark productions, inc.

REHE

CORAL

5TH ANNUAL
ACADEMY
of
COUNTRY MUSIC
AWARDS

COUNTRY
MUSIC'S
PARTY
OF THE YEAR®

MGM GRAND GARDEN ARENA
LAS VEGAS NEVADA
APRIL 18TH 2010

ACM
Academy of Country Music

10th ANNUAL AWARDS
WEDNESDAY, MAY 10, 1995
UNIVERSAL STUDIOS HOLLYWOOD
8:00 PM
ADMIT ONE
VOID IF DETACHED

AC
COU
★ Aw
UNIVER
TUESDAY

0553
VIOLET

EVENT CODE   SECTION/AISLE   ROW/BOX   SEAT
$ 0.00 ORCH   DOOR 15
PRICE
SEC 9
SECTION/AISLE
CA 26x
BB   5
ROW/BOX SEAT

THE UNIVERSAL AM
ACADEMY OF COUN
30th ANNUAL
DRS. CLOSE 4:30PM